The Difference in Butterflies

✦

A Chinese dancer's memoir of her flight from inner and outer tyranny

Marilyn Meeske Sorel
& Yung Yung Tsuai

iUniverse, Inc.
New York Lincoln Shanghai

The Difference in Butterflies
A Chinese dancer's memoir of her flight from inner and outer tyranny

iUniverse books may be ordered through booksellers or by contacting:

iUniverse
2021 Pine Lake Road, Suite 100
Lincoln, NE 68512
www.iuniverse.com
1-800-Authors (1-800-288-4677)

Because of the dynamic nature of the Internet, any Web addresses or links contained in this book may have changed since publication and may no longer be valid.

The views expressed in this work are solely those of the author and do not necessarily reflect the views of the publisher, and the publisher hereby disclaims any responsibility for them.

ISBN: 978-0-595-47325-0 (pbk)
ISBN: 978-0-595-91602-3 (ebk)

Printed in the United States of America

This memoir is dedicated to Martin Lerner & Tysan

We have to find our place in the universe in order to forgive

For Tiffany & Eve

Contents

ACKNOWLEDGMENTS

We are grateful to Phyllis Gangel Jacob, Peri St. Pierre, Johanna Demetrakas, Wayne Furman, Sarah Heller, Kate Amend, Amy Nederlander and Norvie Bullock, for their insight and support.

PART I
MADE IN TAIWAN

This island of green is like a boat
Rocking in my heart
Girl, you are like the boat
Rocking

Let the voice of my song
Be carried by the gentle breeze
Blows open your window curtain

Let my love
Ride over the flowing water
Murmur at your bosom

The long leaves of the palm tree
Can't curl up my love for you
Girl, why do you insist
To be silent
Not responding to my call

This island of green is like a boat
Rocking in my heart

(Rumored to be written by a captured Communist spy)

Intro

1955 Taipei

A seven-year-old child dressed in an elaborate costume, wearing a heavy, glittering headdress stands alone in the middle of a large stage. She faces a performance hall filled with Chiang Kai-shek's soldiers, military officials and party members. The child is patiently awaiting her cue to perform the 'Peace Drum Dance'. She inhales the collective stink of harsh cigarette smoke and foul body odor mixed with an uneasy eagerness to watch a little girl dance. A wave of nausea rushes through her petite body. The presences of Teacher Li, her dance mentor, as well as her parents, do not comfort her. She is locked into an invisible cage. There is a long way to go before she is to be let out of this private prison. First, she performs then she waits for her mother or father to bring her before the generals and other military officials. The men have no problem complimenting the little dancer. And she is passed about to be petted and pinched by them.

Maybe this is the moment her parents will say they are proud of her? She waits. There is always this expectation, but it never seems to happen. There is a reward however, it is a special meal of soymilk, fried dough and flat sesame pancakes. The child eats as her parents (charlatans that they are) discuss her performance. As she is not permitted to express a thought or a feeling she eats and eats until she throws everything up. Her parents laugh at their little star's 'silliness'. And as they laugh fear replaces the food that was in the child's stomach and later a gnarling sensation replaces the fear. And the little dancer will choke ever so quietly in an effort to catch her breath.

My name is Yung Yung Tsuai-Lerner. I was that 'little dancer'. And I remained locked in the invisible cage for nearly twenty years. All the time I had been a faithful witness to my family's sorrow and struggle. I supported them in every way, yet I was denied a voice: 'girls do not have a Chinese voice.' I wallowed in their authoritarian restrictions. For example, I knew Chiang Kai-shek was our president. But I began to pretend I did not know. So I played dumb. Is this what my parents wanted? Their little girl who had no voice but a smiling face? I could

3

no longer speak clearly. I developed a stutter. I squinted my eyes. No one cared I had lost my voice or that I wore near-sighted glasses.

What I could never have imagined was that one of my jailors would become my liberator, would open the cage and let me fly away. My freedom came about unexpectedly like a tidal wave with all the consequences of such a natural disaster.

The USA Information Center at the American Embassy in Taipei gave a workshop on American modern dance history. It was there I was to watch Dancer's World, a documentary on the great American modern dancer Martha Graham. I was struck by the Graham dancers simplicity and elegance. I began to dream of studying this new form of dance with Martha Graham in America. What if I lived a new life, free of family oppression? That is, if I were someone else. Truth was I had no guts to be on my own. It was there I met William Carter, an American dancer who had worked with both New York City Ballet and Martha Graham. He was on tour in Taiwan and came to the Center for rehearsals. Neither of us spoke the other's language but our meeting was my first taste of magic. He observed I had an unusual ability to absorb movement along with a photographic memory which allowed me to copy complex dance movements. Bill sparked a sense of creative individuality in my heart. After he returned to New York this self-awakening, perversely, triggered a depression. I was disgusted every time I saw photos of myself in the TV guide or in a magazine. I needed to separate myself from my parents who I began to hold responsible for my 'fraudulent' existence.

One day I received a letter from Bill informing me Martha Graham would be taking her holiday in Asia. She would be in Taipei such and such a day and he was eager for us to meet. Right away Mother took me to a tailor. And an outfit was created. I was able to show up at Martha's hotel suite dressed in a gold silk tunic, cut to the knees, with purple bell-bottom trousers designed in such a way as to make me appear taller. I felt ridiculous in this absurd costume but the sensation of the sleek silk fabric rubbing against my skin gave me courage.

The China Grand was a luxurious hotel on top of the Yang Ming Mountain. Once inside her suite, the world turned for me. Martha wore a black silk Chinese blouse with matching trousers. Her hair was piled up on her head. She had a high forehead and piercing dark eyes. She darkened her eyes deeper with heavy black eye liner and mascara, adding more drama. Her lips were full and pouty. When she smiled, the lips stretched tightly over beautiful white teeth. She resembled an ancient Egyptian goddess. There was no warmth only power. She was the Queen. I bowed deeply to her with a frightened heart. And, finally, she emitted a faint glow of warmth.

I had arrived with a translator who became increasingly impatient with my shyness in front of the amazing foreign ghost. Her style was sharp and angular, versus my persona, round and laid-back. (As it would turn out, in years to come, her technique was not my sensibility. However, out of loyalty to her I did become one of the more accomplished teachers of the Graham technique.)

Martha ordered tea. Her rich resonant voice, the words strung together in a heavenly music, made my heart skip a beat. She invited me to sit down beside her. She referred to me as 'Marguerite', (my made up English name.) And it was Marguerite who was offered a full personal scholarship, over a cup of Jasmine tea.

She asked if I had had any modern dance training. I explained my work was primarily in Chinese opera and folk dance. She admitted her technique was difficult, requiring strength and diligent study. I answered I would do my best. I pretended I was next to on my way to New York City. "You shouldn't live too far away from the school," she advised, "because traveling is a waste of time and energy." Martha's words 'traveling is a waste of time and energy' beat against my ears. I was thinking inviting me to New York was like inviting me to the moon …

One

I was born September 8th, 1948, the year of the Rat, in Nanjing, China. I was one month old when we fled from the Communist Revolution. We left Nanjing and traveled south. We lived briefly in Hang Chow, then Canton and then Macao. My brother Ping was born in Macao in 1950. We escaped the next year.

The boat took us from Macao to Hong Kong to Taiwan. It floated on the China Sea for a week. While Mother and Father slept, I threw up. Ping would feed himself and me raisins given by a fellow lying next to us. Instead of my mouth, Ping fed raisins to my hair. When we debarked, Mother had to chop off my hair.

Yung Yung is the word for peonies. The flower symbolizes beauty and wealth. One of my dreams was to work in a luxurious flower garden with bountiful colors, a splendid aroma circling around me. I would plant, weed and prune. I would watch the beauty and wealth grow in abundance. When there was fighting, bigotry and war going on I envisioned myself conversing with the little green men who danced under the bushes. They would take me to a fresh meadow where deer leapt across rivers and birds flew through blue clouds. I would sing "Over the Rainbow" like Dorothy. Instead I would become buried in dancing activities not eager for approval from the audience but from my parents.

Both Chiang Kai-shek and Mao Zedong were tyrannical. Mao led the Communist Party and took over Mainland China in 1949. He caused the majority of Chinese to live in pain and suffering. He wiped out the Tibetan culture massacring most of them. Mao created massive famine during the 1950's and dictated the so called Cultural Revolution during the 1960's. Millions had died under his mad control. We were lucky to escape. Nonetheless if Chiang Kai-shek was a benevolent dictator why did we lack free choice, spiritual guidance and an intelligent way of living?

Taiwan is an island on the subtropical equator shaped like a crescent moon floating between the China Sea and the Pacific Ocean. Taipei City is a basin surrounded by small hills. Snow exists in the elevated mountain peaks where wild animals run loose. This idea appealed to me.

The Dutch pirates called it Formosa, the beautiful island, later, the Chinese renamed it Taiwan, plateau in the sea. Centuries ago, most habitants were aborigines. By the end of the fifteenth century, Zheng Chen Gong, a general of late Ming Dynasty had ordered his troops to retreat from Fujian province to Taiwan across China Sea. The people who followed Zheng Chen Gong were Han people loyal to Ming imperials. After pushing the aborigines further to the deep mountains, they had settled in clusters within the valleys and by the seaports. They had resisted the occupation of Manchuria until the emperor Qing Kangxi (1622–1772) invaded Taiwan. While many were slaughtered, others submitted to the rule of Manchuria. However, after the Boxer Rebellion in the late Eighteen Hundred's, Empress Dowager of Manchuria was pressured to give Taiwan to Japan. The Empress Dowager made an infamous speech referring to Taiwan as an island of 'no bird sings tunes and no flower smells fragrance'. The Taiwanese made a noble attempt to resist the Japanese invasion, only to be massacred. At the end of World War II, Taiwan was returned to Mainland China.

So this was our destiny.

We first lived in a shack with other families in Keelun City, a seaport town north of Taipei. A few wooden boards mixed with clay were put together on a slanted hillside. There was one electric light bulb hanging from the ceiling. The weather was cold and wet. The chilling air beat at our skin and bones day and night. We sat by a coal fire lit in a clay pot. My brother, Ping's fat little hand would clutch my palm. It was the hand of a chubby three-year-old boy, with dimples between the joints of his fingers. I would rub his hand, "Little fatty hand, little fatty hand, papa can't help, mama can't help, little fatty hand, we take care of the world, we will be brave, little fatty hand …" During the summer days, we slept under banana trees. My grandmother's bamboo fan over our heads waved away the mosquitoes.

I had a fear of walking to the outhouse at night. I cried when I had to go. My parents laughed at me. So, I kept crying, with my legs ajar. Cried as I sat and faced the blackness of the mountain's shadow clutching the earth. I envisioned the deep wooded hills engulfing me. Opening my mouth wide, I let out a sound that must have been compressed within my chest for days. The mountain echoed my yells, empowering me as if I were expressing the world's sorrow. Sometimes Ping would join me in the rally.

Winter was bitter, cold and damp. It rained every day during the month of February. Clouds gathered in various shapes and forms, compressing a small and condensed land below. We waited until March for the sun to shine. The sun broke through in spring. Gentle easy breezes swept through the island, awakening our senses. Rhododendrons and Peach blossoms colored the mountain slopes. Then, it was hot and humid over the summer. The blazing sun beat on our backs. The air hard to breathe. To live meant to sweat. The summer could feel long and stretched out … October brought a fresh gusty whispering wind. The sky looked high and the air felt open. By November we would begin to buy sweaters, light jackets and rain coats for the oncoming winter. This is how we experienced our new world.

◆   ◆   ◆

According to Chinese mythology, the empress Chang Er lived thirty-five hundred years ago in the Shai Dynasty. Her husband, Ho-Yee, shot down ten suns and saved the world. However, he perpetuated war and destruction throughout the earth. Out of her sadness and despair over her husband's misdeed, she took a magic potion and flew to the Moon. Many centuries later during the Tang Dynasty, the emperor Tang Ming Huang, who was also a poet, a musician and a dancer, had a dream he visited the Moon Goddess, Chang Er. She taught him how to fly using streams of ribbons. Upon awakening, he composed music and choreographed The Ribbon Dance.

◆   ◆   ◆

When I dreamed of becoming a dancer, I leaped over mountains, glided through clouds, flew upon a peacock feather, waved golden leaves at the sun. I twirled in the world's wind, wove among stars. I swung my sword and slashed the nine-headed dragon. I tumbled down the deep sea, swam with the daughters of the Ocean King. I rocked and wriggled in the blazing flames, hopped and jumped from tree to tree. When I stood still, the universe would rotate around me. That was the stuff of my dreams so far away from my future encounter with the great modern dancer Martha Graham which would change my Chinese life.

We were brave souls. My parents were broken financially and emotionally. Day after day they struggled for survival. They had lost their homes, their hearts and their spirits. They tended to live in the past, dreaming of their lost childhood. Father was twenty-nine and Mother twenty-four, carrying two young children and a middle-aged widowed mother. Their lives were consumed by the gnarling sensation left from psychic trauma which was how I caught it. Surrounded by an ocean of fear, anger and desperation, my parents laughed when their daughter cried. Soon my tears stopped. They gathered in my heart to form the lotus pond of my dreams. Dreams I did not share. Dreams that might never be realized.

Green army trucks lined the streets, soldiers displaying guns. Because we were Mandarin refugees we were taken for spies. We were watched. In those years we lived in terror, people were convicted for no reason. We never knew if China was going to bomb us. Chiang Kai-shek took a small piece of the terror pie and left the larger one to Mao. Our communities of Mandarin refugees were treated like dirty dogs. There were no visas, no passports for us. My parents so dominated my life it never occurred to me there were other cultures, other societies. There was no sense of an outside world. I lived in a dark corner of the Universe sitting at the family knee listening to fox stories, ghost tales and Father's ongoing declarations about returning home to China. Taiwan was closed off. No exit. We were in lock-down.

One day the radio announced that thousands of Chinese prisoners of war in Korea had pleaded for political asylum in Taiwan. The Korean War was fought between North and South Korea, actually it was really an international war fought between the Russians and the Chinese vs. the Americans. The Chinese government used the method of "human wave attacks". They sent millions of men to Korea fighting against the American's heavy gun powers. Male bodies, aged from fifteen to forty five were trapped in Korea "to honor the principles of the people". Some of the men did not understand these principles they were supposed to fight for, while others did not care. They were captured by the American soldiers and became prisoners of war. So, they asked to go to Taiwan. The Taiwanese government did receive them with outrageous news headlines for their own political agenda.

Mother went down to the docks to look for her brother. She waited. The water brought ship after ship of shadow figures. The air breezed with the sound of cries and joy. Families united; lovers embraced; husbands and wives screamed aloud. She watched parents and sons prostrate to thank heaven and the gods of fortune while she remained silent. After the dock emptied, she refused to go home. Father stayed by her. They held each other like petrified stones.

At home Mother no longer smiled, she no longer talked, she ate when she was told to and drank when she was handed a glass. Ping would look at me with frightened eyes. He knew not to cry. He was three years old but he knew silent pain by heart. I held his hand tight, folding his frightened eyes inside of my hands. I tried to comfort Ping, but my fear was also great. I chanted my song of "Little fatty hand", hoping we might be brave enough to fight against the gnarling sensation spreading in the air.

We sat in that shack surrounded by a few wooden boards like animals waiting for the slaughter. We sat with our teeth clenched, sweeping our tears aside. Mother mourned for her brother; I mourned for Mother. Then I stood up and walked out of the shack with Ping, chanting my favorite tune,"Little fatty hand, little fatty hand …" We walked to the woods. First banana trees, next a jungle of bamboo, after that vast amount of pine trees. We kept on walking. I kept on chanting until we were exhausted. Finally, we found a spot to lie down. Sleeping against the musty earth, under the sky, nothing seemed to matter. We slept for the human psyche to heal.

I do not remember how we returned home or when Mother recovered from her depression. She did lift her head up one day. Her queer sense of humor had returned. It sparkled in her eyes. She reminded us of our neighbor Mr. Lin in Macao who had a little cat. She said one morning they stepped outside their room and there was the cat's head and skin hung by the wall. Mr. Lin had killed the cat and ate it the night before. "And," she said impishly, "That's how your father has become allergic to cats."

We lived in Keelun for two years. Everyday I prayed to the Goddess of Mercy, Quan Yin. I asked her to help my parents to fulfill their hopes of returning home to Mainland China. I was obsessed by their 'unhappiness'. I wished only to please them.

Despite our harsh living condition, Father would take us to the Chinese opera houses or the movie theaters on weekends. We would travel four hours on a train to Taipei City once a week for this outing.

The movie theater was dark. The audience respectful, as if we were watching sacred Chinese opera. We brought our own thermos of hot green tea, bottles of Coke-Cola, tangerines, peanuts, pickled eggs and watermelon seeds. We sang along with the actors on screen and when they spoke we would make comments about the plot and the acting. Someone in the audience might burst out in argument with a character. The children played hide and seek behind the wooden seats. Babies wore diapers with openings to pee or poo whenever they had the urge to do so. Men would spit out watermelon seeds. Orange peels and eggshells were scattered on the ground. This was how we disappeared from our lives. We watched the Wizard of Oz five times. We cheered when Dorothy clicked her red shoes. Mother and I fell in love with Judy Garland. At home she helped me to set up a corner. Red bricks were stacked under a wooden board next to Grandma's bed. There I had my paper dolls, the miniature tin cups and spoons, hand made clay houses with furniture. On the wall, above the board we tacked a poster of Dorothy and friends. I conversed with them whenever I felt troubled.

◆　　◆　　◆

1953 was a humid summer. The smell of the banana trees sprouting from the moist earth was heavy in the air. Beads of sweat pulled through thin layers of cotton sleeveless shirts. Most people were half naked, lazily waving their bamboo fans. They sat on the wooden stools in the courtyard. I often danced in circles. They would laugh, shaking their fans in rhythm. They told me I had talent. I ought to take some dance lessons and become a movie star. I could make my family rich. I was five years old.

So I was not surprised the day Mother dressed me up in new white cotton dress, with a pink satin bow tied at the back of my waist. My hair tightly pulled into two ponytails above my ears. I walked out of our shack with Mother, wearing the uncomfortable black shiny shoes. A paddy cab was waiting for us by the street corner. We were on our way to Taipei City, to my first dance class.

There were more than twenty girls in the class, each one like me dressed in white. It was a huge room with a splendid wood floor, large mirrors and several long polished wooden bars mounted along the walls. While we waited for the teacher, I walked over to the bar. I tried to imitate a student practicing at the bar, hopping in the same fashion, up and down, bending my knees.

I instantly broke down in tears when the teacher entered the room. Girls bowed to her, "How are you, Teacher Li." My body stiffened. She held a stick in her hand and a broad smile on her face while she stretched her arms above us. She appeared to me hard and strict. Her full head of black hair was piled up on top of her. She wore bright red lipstick glamorously framing her striking white teeth. She was in her late thirties, older than my parents. She was very dramatic, yelling, smiling, and teasing us. I was frightened. I sensed danger, as if she would sacrifice children for her art. In my tiny eyes, she looked tall and full. I held my tears in my congested chest, taking the lesson from her. She taught us to puff our chests up in proud gestures.

Every other day, I took lessons from Teacher Li. I followed her instructions faithfully. The first an hour and a half we studied classical ballet. We held onto the barre and learned plies, tendues, ports de bras, degage, ronds de jambe, frappe, passé, develope, grand battement and so on. In the center floor, we were taught different directions, combinations, adage, pirouette turns, fouette, and petit allegro jumps, such as glissades, sautés, changements, sisonnes, jetes, tempsleves, and assembles. And then we crossed the floor with step combinations, walks, chaines, leaps and grand allegro, such as grand jetes, grand jete en tournant, etc. After the ballet exercises, we learned repertoire dances for an additional hour. I sweated and panted in every class. Some days I mastered the control of muscle coordination with great pride. Other days I lost my concentration for whatever I was supposed to do, then Teacher Li would become stern, rolling her eyes, ignoring me for the entire class. Regardless what happened in class, I loved dancing. Teacher Li was difficult to please. She was impatient. Her screams frightened me. When she shouted, I thought she must be a very unhappy woman. But she did praise me. I had to admit despite her hysterics, she made me feel proud, especially when I was asked to demonstrate certain movements in front of my classmates.

The repertoire works were Ballet, Chinese folk and opera dances. Teacher Li taught me many solo performances. I began spending more and more time at the dance school. During the classes, I had a sense of flying. My parents worshipped Teacher Li. Both of them accompanied me to every class, where they would intensely observe me. There was warmth between Teacher Li and my parents. They seemed to understand each other. At times, I wished I could be included in their circle of smiles, but I was a child. I realized my parents had desires in their heart. They wanted me to be a child star. Soon Father became the chairman of the Parents Teacher Association, raising funds and organizing events for Teacher Li. Mother went over every detail of my dance steps at home.

At the end of the year, Teacher Li was giving a recital at the City Hall. We had beautiful costumes. I was given a major solo part to be performed in front of hundreds of people. During the dress rehearsals I felt the bright lights on me. I was the star.

At last the day came. We were crowded in a small dressing room. Mother spent two hours making me up. Layer upon layer of facial foundation mixed with powder were applied, then red and pink rouge on the cheeks, brown eye shadow, black eye liner, with the final touch of brilliant red lipstick. I discovered my legs had fallen asleep. I moved slowly out of the chair to stretch my muscles. At that moment, I imagined I had become Grandma and contracted her arthritis in the blink of two hours.

The opening act included everyone dancing in a circle. This went well. Back in the dressing room, I sat in front of a mirror sipping from a bottle of Coca-Cola. I looked at the mirror. My face remained powdered ivory white, the cheeks still brushed in crimson red. My eyebrows were shaped to look like crescent moons, two black arches, my eyes deepened by blackened eyelashes. It was a fascinating face. An amazing face. I marveled how Mother had transformed me from a plain girl to a magazine beauty. I was falling in love with the face in the mirror. I was Dorothy clicking her crimson shoes.

"Yung Yung," a loud sharp voice called out. I woke up. The dressing room had emptied. The girl who stood next to me in the dancing circle came through the door with a sneer on her face, her hands in the air. "Solo part, all gone! You missed it!" she said.

Mother rushed in and swapped me on the head. She was furious. More people drifted in. Some of them smiled and some frowned. I had missed my grand solo entrance.

Father was my booker. Mother was Father's messenger. She faithfully carried out his frustrations and anger. It would take years for me to separate them, to be able to see them as individuals.

I did not have to wait much longer to perform solo. The following month I went on stage holding a bamboo basket and proceeded to glide through an invisible door. There, I sat on a bright, Chinese red stool performing the Embroidery Dance. I jumped up in reaction to being pricked by a needle. Another time I mimed an old woman having trouble threading the needle. I draped the silk over my shoulders as in a fitting. By the end, I gracefully danced while throwing the silk into the air creating a lyrical tableau with body and fabric.

Teacher Li, who had been born in Taiwan, had studied dance in Japan. She was a well-known dancer and teacher in Taiwan by the time I entered her school. She often invited famous Chinese opera dancers and Japanese Ballerinas to be guest teachers. A year later, I was chosen to learn 'Peace Drum Dance'. My parents were thrilled.

Teacher Li had choreographed this dance during a trip to America. The Peace Drum dance had originated in North East China, a Manchuria territory. It was chosen to be performed in a dance competition to celebrate "peace". Father was beside himself with anxiety. Teacher Li swayed her torso and stomped her feet. She would yell, "Smile! Mei Mei! (Chinese word for little sister) Smile!"

We entered the National Folk Dance Competition, which was held in a huge sport arena. Three thousand people in the audience were cheering for us. The dance adopted a Tango rhythm. Slow, slow, quick, quick, quick. A duet pattern weaved in and out of a figure eight. The dance repeated the same musical patterns seven times, each time we ran faster than before. Our costumes were elaborate: Chungseng tops, vests and drawstring pants, embroidered with beaded dragons and phoenix figures. I wore peach my partner apple green. The rabbit, fur collars were high around the neck. Our long black braids flew on our backs while we twirled. Strong Chinese Opera style movement with our heels down first, then rolling onto toes. The dancers were required to use their legs in agile muscular manipulations. Holding an oval shaped flat drum on the left hand and a curved bamboo stick on the right, the girls beat out its rhythm: Dum Dum dum dum dum. Dum Dum dum dum dum, dum dum dum, dum dum dum, Dum Dum dum dum dum. By the end of the dance there was an illusion of flying.

I pushed my movements forward from the bottom of my heels, a huge smile on my face. The audience laughed with delight. And we won the competition.

◆   ◆   ◆

One morning Mother awakened us very early. We were moving. She quickly dressed us in brand new clothes; Ping had a starched, pure white, dress shirt, a pair of indigo short pants, white socks and black shoes. He sported a buster brown haircut, which shaped his thick dark hair into a round mop on top of his sweet chubby face. I wore a pink ruffled skirt, pink blouse, pink butterfly bows on my two skimpy pigtails, pink socks and even pink shoes which squeezed my toes. She hustled us outdoors to a paddy-cab. Grandma was already seated wearing her black widow Chungseng dress, her hair combed neatly in a bun.

The Cooli (hard labor man) waited for us. He was smoking a cigarette. His skin and muscles were tanned under a set of white button-down Chungseng shirt. He rolled up his long sleeves high above his elbows. Below his waist, He had a pair of black drawstring pants. He sat on the bicycle seat in front, along with two paddles on the sides. Behind his seat was a carriage for the passengers. Grandma and Ping sat on the vinyl-cushioned seat and I squatted down on the small plywood platform below. I thought oh we're going home at last to Mainland China.

It was a long ride. I had dozed off only to wake up to see more rice paddies. By the time the paddy-cab stopped at noon the three of us were coated with dust, lightly toasted brown dumplings. We had arrived at a new and foreign neighborhood.

There was a narrow wooden door in the center of a cement wall, flat against a small closed-in alley. On the right hand side I saw a tiny rectangular old wooden framed window, which had a worn out plastic curtain. I followed Grandma and entered the door. A shocking odor crawled in my nostril.

Chicken poop was everywhere, thick as a blanket, covering the cold cement floor.

"Where am I going to sleep?" Grandma spoke loudly, hitting her hands against the bamboo bed she was sitting on.

"Where you're sitting," Father said.

"Bad Feng Shui!" Grandma stared at Father.

We jumped up and started to help each other to move the bamboo bed. No matter where we moved, no matter how we tried, it was all bad Feng Shui.

"Our neighbor is a butcher. He has a pig stall next to our house," Father laughed, "we won't ever starve."

Grandma's bed faced the tiny wooden door, which led to an indoor toilet. Plywood was joined to make a small room separate from the rest of the house. Ping and I called it "the Box". It was two by two feet, with a dark hole dug in the middle. We wore wooden clogs when we had to go. We had daily fights over who could stay inside the longest. Maybe it was not as ideal as our granduncle's that had an actual seated toilet with a white tiled bathtub sitting next to it but it would beat the long walk to the outhouse. Sometimes, I was scared squatting in "the Box". I imagined two arms reaching up from the hole pulling me down eating me alive while suffocating in my own shit.

"Don't give me the dark face," Father announced, "You know this is a temporary home. We're going back to our real home next year in Mainland China where tea tastes better and sugar buns are sweeter. I know I will inherit a three-story house with wooden stair railings carved in dragonheads and phoenix tails. Not only will we have our own rooms but a whole suite to each one of you. We will have courtyards and stone gardens. Each year, we will create a hundred foot dragon made of silk and rayon from our very own fabric store. The dragon will dance on the streets during the lantern festival. Wait another year and we'll be home."

Two

Mother decorated the living quarter with five flowery vinyl chairs, a round wooden dining table painted Chinese red and a huge colorful bluish tin basin for our once a week sponge bath. After which I felt like a leaf newly turned with fresh sandalwood soap smells and a scrubbed clean face. On the far side were tile shelves built around three sides with tile panels lining the wall beneath the shelves. A large sink sat in the corner at the end of a shelf. Apparently, the house had been a barbershop before we moved in.

There was another smaller room belonging to my parents just large enough to fit a double bed. Green vines grew in my heart, because little fatty hand Ping got to share the bed with Mother and Father.

Tuesday nights after supper was story night. Father sat on a small bamboo stool soaking his feet in a basin filled with steaming hot water. Ping and I squatted at his feet in anticipation.

Father played with our expectations. He tickled and teased. He squinted his eyes at us before he lifted his chin up, pursed his lips and let out, "Yuwoo …!" He howled with joy as he worked a small hand towel back and forth between his toes in the sizzling water. "Da … Da … Da … Da …!" He expressed his delight with a series of "Da" sounds. Then he began his stories in his soft toned Mandarin speech. The characters that walked out of Father's tales seemed vivid and alive to us. In this way Father believed he was entertaining us.

One of his stories took place in remote rural China. A tiny village sat under the foothill of a mountain. About five hundred feet from the village, there was one communal outhouse. People said it was haunted with ghosts who would go wild. These spirits indulgently partied after midnight. It was said they sacrificed human flesh in exchange for their immortality. So at night no one dared walk through the long black pathway to this dangerous underworld, the outhouse. Everyone had to hold their bodily functions until dawn, father said.

A traveler passed through the village. He was a well-educated scholar, world wise and sophisticated. He sneered at the ignorance of the villagers. He was warned not to go to the outhouse at night. Nevertheless, midnight came; the traveler got the urge and went. Squatting over the hole, he heard people talking gibberish nearby. Fear set in and he hurried out of the outhouse.

It was a long walk back to the farmer's house. He saw a man walking rapidly in front of him. He felt relieved to see another person. He rushed forward to catch up with him.

"I'm glad to have caught up with you. There seems to be ghosts in that outhouse."

"How do you know they are ghosts?" the stranger asked.

"I heard them ..."

"Have you ever seen a ghost?"

"No. But I heard they have no chins ..."

While the scholar spoke the man turned his head. It was a scary face, and his chin was missing. The scholar fainted. Father told us that the unfortunate man disappeared from earth.

Ping and I were equally wowed and frightened by these tales.

◆   ◆   ◆

Monkey King rolled out of a stone. His mission in life was to escort his master, the Buddhist Saint, Tang Xuan Zang. Together they traveled from the emperor's palace to the Western Kingdom of Heaven. On their journey to the west Monkey King fumbled, tumbled and recovered. They faced challenge after challenge from the demons who wanted to devour the Saint's flesh. Finally they reached their destiny. Buddha welcomed them joyfully. They received the sacred Sanskrit scrolls.

◆   ◆   ◆

Father told us there were ghosts of all kinds: Hungry ones, drowned ones, hanged ones, and beheaded ones hiding under the holes in old houses. They reached out to grab our butts. They roamed in wildernesses turning their heads in different directions and showing their twisted faces to frightened wanderers.

Snakes disguised as beautiful maidens crossed the West Lake on a boat. Scorpions and spiders spun their webs; white bone demons sprawled their legs; sea monsters opened their jaws. In the dark caves full of poisonous plants captured human souls. We could not get enough of Father's stories.

◆   ◆   ◆

When I reached the age of six, I preferred to have my hair done in two pony-tails with pink ribbons tied in butterfly knots. I wanted to wear a dress, a white-lace one, to be more feminine. Although everyone told me I looked like Father, I desired to look like Mother, who I thought was graceful and beautiful. I was aware of the differences between men, women, boys and girls. I knew men and women could fall in love, get married and start their own families. I thought growing up was the best thing that could happen to me. I would like to grow up as soon as possible.

I was pretty. I was ready to be a grown-up. When we played on the streets men asked to kiss my cheeks and gave me candies for being pretty. I loved the candies, but had to wipe their kisses off my face. I spent most afternoons in the alley in front of our house. There I met Go Go.

I used to see him on the street. I called him Go Go (older brother). He seemed old to me the way everybody grown-up did. I thought he was so cool with his grown-up hair combed back in shining jet-black oil; his beige khaki pants tightly tied around his waist, a white sleeveless Tee shirt snuggled about his tanned torso. When he walked, he swung his hip side to side, as if he were in a half sleep, strolling in slow motion. His manner was different. He never asked to kiss my cheek. He looked straight into my eyes. He spoke to me with an open and friendly face. I thought when I grow up, I want to be like Go Go, or at least I marry him.

One summer evening, I wandered over to his shed to ask for a ride. I saw him crouched in the dark corner on a bamboo stool, his body curled up. I hoped to see his smile and friendly face. He sat motionless on the stool, tears running down his face. He did not see me. I was frightened. Grown-ups don't cry. I ran out and stumbled over a stone. He did not come to help me. He remained crying like a two-year old boy. I went home disappointed.

The next morning, there was a lot of commotion out on the street. I was hoping to see Go Go, his black hair flying, his khaki pants shifting and his bicycle shining. I was hoping to see his bright smile, his white teeth. I was hoping to hear him apologize for not taking me for a ride. I wanted to hold onto his midriff, sit tightly against his warm back. But he was not there. I wanted to change into my prettiest precious white dress and come out to the street to greet him. I wanted to ask Mother to sponge and soak me in the freshest sandalwood soap so I would smell good and look nice. I longed to see Go Go's swinging hip walk in slow motion.

Our neighbor Lee Mama (Chinese way of addressing an older woman) said, "What a shame, only sixteen years old."

"What happened?" I did not understand.

"Go Go, he hanged himself in the outhouse last night." Lee Mama gave me a sharp look. I was in a panic. The damned outhouse was cursed with ghosts, foxes and monsters! Creatures from the underworld crept through the dark holes snatching our beloved.

"What do you mean he hanged … himself?" I asked.

"He killed himself! He's dead!" Lee Mama screamed at me.

"Dead?"

"He was merely a student with no school to go to!" Lee Mama was furious, "Damn the government! Damn the politics! Damn the wars! Damn anyone who wants to take over this country! We suffer, the useless, little people. We lose our homes, our family. We have to live in this damned, hopeless place. We have got to see young people kill themselves. Heaven has the eyes and Heaven can see the evil Karma. His mother will weep until her eyes bleed, sending a son to an island to kill himself. Better if the Communists kill him. At least he'd have his home dirt thrown on his grave …"

I ran to his shed. I sat by his bed. A worn suitcase was leaning against a wall, and his bicycle slanting next to it. A hot water thermos, a small glass cup, a ceramic rice bowl and a pair of wooden chopsticks lay scattered on the cement floor.

I did not know why it was so important for me to see, but I wanted to make sure I would remember his house. In a panic I ran to "the Box" to check that the hole was there and no hand was coming out and I needed to be assured I would not vanish in a puff. I searched for Go Go. Maybe he will walk out of thin air and smile at me.

A red rage began to burst from me, as if our Chinese red dining table had been shoved down my throat and exploded.

Go Go, how dare you leave me? How dare you not grow old and wise, as you seemed to promise? How dare you disappear in a flash?

◆   ◆   ◆

It was rumored Teacher Li's husband was a gambler and a womanizer. She was supporting her teen-age son, as well as her teen-age brother and sister. On top of that she had adopted a young daughter, about three or four years old. The little girl stayed aloof, far in the corner. I never even knew her name. Father often expressed his desire for Teacher Li to adopt me as well. "Crazy idea," Mother said, "we are Mandarins and she a Taiwanese."

One day, when I was about ten, I was having lunch with Teacher Li. Her husband entered the dining room to present her with a gift. He wore a guilty, pleading smile. She turned her head away and slammed down her chopsticks. He walked out of the room. Teacher Li turned to me, "Who bought him a motorcycle? Who paid for this big house? I did. How dare he carry my assistant, Miss Huang on his motorcycle all over town?"

Eventually she fired Miss Huang. Soon afterwards, Teacher Li's husband gambled away her dance school and house. She was forced to move out and to divorce. It was the first time I saw Teacher Li vulnerable. She was angry and hurt. I did not know what to say to her. Although she never expected me to respond, she related to me as an object, or as I would come to understand later, as merchandise. We finished our meal in silence. Afterwards, Teacher Li took out her make up kit. She applied thick cream over her face, which fascinated me. She told me she was going to take a nap. She said I could sleep with her if I wished. I shook my head and ran up to the roof to play with her son, who was considerably older than me. I thought Teacher Li had children of her own, plus an adopted child. How generous to take on further personal responsibilities, a seeming kindness, contrary to the severe character of her teaching persona.

Over a bowl of Wanton soup at our house, my parents promised to help her start a new dance school. Meanwhile, I performed on every weekend. My picture showed up in newspapers and magazines. Although it had become a subtle burden to my heart. Performing to large audiences was no longer fun. I had to watch every movement I made, on stage as well as off. My parents watched me like hawks, criticizing whenever there was an imperfection. I wondered who was Yung Yung? A performer with a fake smile? Or the little girl who turned melancholy most of the time? Father rarely came home before midnight. He was absorbed in Teacher Li's new dance studio. It hurt to see the energized look on father's face when he saw Teacher Li. I was upset. I kept my emotions to myself. I would never dare to openly react, never dare to ask Father. Mother seemed to withdraw. She rarely smiled. One day I found a poem she had written. It began with the line, *"Cold, cold, cold/My heart has turned into a stone/Loneliness accompanies me into my bedroom/Turning my life from sweet to bitter/I have given my love to the very person/Who has changed his heart/Cold is all I can feel/Cold is all"*

One hot afternoon I awakened abruptly from a strange dream while taking a nap. A crush of rose ash permeated the dance studio. The rich perfume clung to my nostrils. I twirled off the cot. I faced the large mirror. Instead of seeing my image I saw a silvery woman's smooth naked body quivering, smoking up the mirror. It was Teacher Li! Her small round breasts looked moist and their nipples extended like tiny rosy fingertips. She began to sway, to dance. I was sleepwalking and hallucinating. Father appeared out of nowhere and shook me awake. I asked him why he was there. He said he was working in the new studio. The effect of the dream disappeared quickly like my other apparitions.

◆   ◆   ◆

For eight years we remained in this house of chicken shit and pig cries. Ping and I grew taller while Father's voice grew softer. Ping began a life of trouble at school as well as around the neighborhood. While I received the first prize for the National Folk Dance Competition, Ping flunked at school.

When I turned thirteen we moved to a new house a few blocks away. It was not to Father's ancestral house in China. Although we had a separate dining room and a new western style bathroom, with seated toilet and a bathtub.

The first day Ping and I took a luxuriously long bath. The family gathered around the dining table where Mother shared a secret. "Aiyeh! I feel so relieved. We're no longer in that house." And then she told us it was haunted. The barber had murdered his mistress there.

"Bad Feng Shui," I said. Making a Chinese joke. I spoke out of turn. A roaring laughter tumbled out of my mouth. Ping started to laugh as well. We laughed so hard, we startled our parents. To my surprise, Grandma was laughing with us.

At the break of dawn, Ping and I began the day practicing Tai Chi Chuan with Father in our backyard. The tiny brown sparrows fluttered their wings, singing familiar tunes. Banana trees stood tall and proud, flirtatiously intermingling with orange and pineapple trees. The air wafted humid smells, sweet and melancholy. There was a vegetable garden next to us, with rows of green plants sprouting from Mother Earth. The vegetation appeared to be laughing in the morning sun. The red brick walls around the green wooden houses added pleasure to our awakened senses.

When we finished a round of Tai Chi Chuan, we sat down at table for breakfast. We had rice soup steaming hot with little dried fish, fried peanuts, pickled cabbage and sautéed green vegetables.

After we ate Ping and I dipped our feet in the streams and threw pebbles at each other. A curvy winding road displayed its bareness. On the left side of the road, bundles of dry hay dispersed here and there, mixing with patches of vegetable gardens and piles of brownish dirt; on the right side, there was a small stream, which farmers had dug for the water source of their rice field; beyond the stream, rice paddies widened the landscape into a wilderness of rolling hills. The rice paddies created a rich landscape. The palm, banana and orange trees were in abundance. But it was the bamboo forests, which lured people to dream. Poets praised the blossoms of the rhododendrons and musicians sang for the island of green.

We did not question how we arrived in paradise. I was enraptured by the rice paddy stretching for miles. A wet, green mirage on the side of a pebbled gravel path. On those paths children hopped side to side, playfully dashing forward and back. They laughed and sang popular military marching songs, with their beige school bags and black and white uniforms, a tin lunch box containing mostly rice and vegetables strapped on the side of their waists. Sparrows flew overhead; bicycles were speeding by; occasionally a water buffalo waggling its tail followed farmer boys dressing in traditional Mandarin collar, "Peng Qao" buttons, "Chungseng" shirts, drawstring pants rolled up knee high. The conical shaped bamboo straw hats helped protect from the flaming sun. This memory of my brother's laughter, his yells and cries fill me with joy. For a while it was a childhood of uncontested innocence.

◆   ◆   ◆

Teacher Li taught me numerous solo dances. I would accompany her to theaters and performing halls. I was about nine when she marched us to a basketball stadium in Taipei City. We were to perform that evening. On arrival the group of noisy children instantly dispersed. The enormous expanse of space excited me. I began to cartwheel along the floor. 1,2,3 … 17,18 … 26 … 28. I made twenty-eight cartwheels in one breath. I was on top of the mountain; the rotating universe was under my feet. I was close to God. I thought the stage would definitely be my power spot.

My performances became my parents' hopes and dreams. Father's enthusiasm for my dance career had become an obsession. He seemed equally consumed by the needs of Teacher Li's school. This was the start of Mother fading away. She would come to my performances. She would make me up with pride, but I could tell her heart and spirit was missing. What's wrong? Mother?

Truth was, there had been no outside world until Teacher Li. A few years later Teacher Li left Taiwan. I surprised myself by bursting out in sobs at the sight of Teacher Li in the airport, saying goodbye.

I listened to Grandma's whispered humming of ancient China: a fox song; Mother's silence in her bitterness: a mute song; Father belted out Chinese operas: a roaring song and Ping's angry protest: a drummer-boy song. Most of all, whenever and wherever we went, Taipei City blasted out her military marching sounds.

Chinese operas were alive and active in Father's world, but Mother went for American Hollywood musical movies. Father took us to see Chinese Beijing operas every weekend while Mother worshipped Judy Garland and Fred Astaire. Along with Western classical music and Chinese pop songs, radio stations would broadcast military slogans and marching songs.

I had a passion for drums since I was five. Rhythmic beating sounds beguiled my body and soul. They helped me express my bottled up energy. One afternoon after class, I followed a teacher into the musical instrument closet. I wanted to play the drums alone. The teacher did not see me. She locked the door behind her. Eventually, I fell asleep. My parents looked for me in vain. Finally the teacher went back to the school and found me sleeping on the floor besides my drums.

Later, the flute fascinated me. Lyrical soothing calming sounds closer to heaven. I joined the school band, soon to be discharged because I did not have the discipline and time to practice. Dance was my principle occupation. My body became my musical instrument.

If Father's stories entertained us with the unknown, Mother's stories rang of realism. Each time the version was altered. But the vacant stare in her eyes remained the same. Ping and I felt we did not quite play up to the supporting roles in her drama. We were extras, mere stage props before her.

One of the stories was about feeding an infant. "Ayih! Those damned wretched Western doctors. They told me to feed the baby two ounces of Western formula per day. The baby cried day and night. She was so tiny. Her face looked like a little white fox, with bulging eyes and pointed mouth. She reminded me of a chicken with its feathers plucked. My mother had to tie the baby to the earth with a red string around her ankle during the full moon banquet given to the newborn baby.

"After we hired a wet nurse, she blew up like a balloon, with those chubby cheeks. I wanted to eat her round belly.

"Ayih! That wretched wet nurse! She starved the baby when we were so poor in Macao; when the baby was about a year and half, the wet nurse knew her milk had dried up, but she wouldn't tell us. She robbed us with the gold we paid her.

What Karma. I heard she was hung and beaten to death by her neighbors for her gold and jewelry.

"We took the baby to the hospital everyday. The doctor gave her intravenous B12. Well, I didn't know the Western medicine from sugar to salt. I was carrying Ping in my belly like a watermelon. I was starving, too. Some days, I'd munch on crackers to stop my hunger. But I dragged my feet to the hospital. The nurses crowded around and played with the baby. She entertained even then.

"It had been an entire year. We were worried. Death seemed to be waiting for us around every corner. The Iron Curtain fell on the border of Macao, Hong Kong and Taiwan. We were uncertain about our fate. We sat silent. Midnight crept in.

"Then the spoiled child let out cranky cries. Her irritating sobs broke through the silence and her ill temper pierced the night so deep. She was two years old. She didn't know how high the heaven could reach and how low the earth could crawl. The child's indulgence enraged her father. He picked her up with force. He carried her out to the courtyard. It was a night so dark and still. There was no moonlight crossing our windowsills and there was no crickets chirping about in our unsettled minds. The courtyard gave out a fox song, luring us to an unknown world.

"A well was sitting in the center of the courtyard, monstrously deep underground, snaking into the earth. The well's mouth opened waiting for a feast.

"I heard shouting from the courtyard. Stop crying! Stop crying or I'll throw you down the well! I tiptoed to the open door, peeked out at the moonless courtyard. I saw the little child being held upside down. Her head dipped in the mouth of the well. I thought I saw something come alive, a dark force coming out of the well upward, trying to devour the baby. A quiet child won't get punished, I told my heart. Fortunately the man turned and came home with the baby intact."

Many days, I would sit side by side with Ping on small bamboo stools helping Grandma to sift sand out of rice. Mother would lean against the red dining table chopping up a chunk of meat. She would wave the meat cleaver in the air, as she told the story about the baby, over and over again. It was not until I was ten years old that I realized mother's baby story was about me.

In 1945, my mother, Kang Lin Wang was nineteen. She was living in Wuhu City, Anhui province in China. That year the United States dropped an atom bomb on Hiroshima. The earth bled; the wind cried; the world lamented—and Japan surrendered. Surreptitiously, the Chinese people set off firecrackers and whispered the news; for the victory had come so fast everyone was still in shock. Besides, fear of the Japanese soldiers among townsfolk remained and rumors ran rampant: fortunetellers' heads should be chopped off. How could they not have foreseen Japan losing the war? It was a miracle, for had the Japanese soldiers just yesterday gone about in perfectly pressed uniforms, their boots shining and spotless, and their rifles sparkling and ready to kill?

Eight years of war, in terror and pain was suddenly over, but the memory of Nanjing massacre continued. Japanese soldiers could lose their heads again and strike out violently at any bystander. If that happened, would anyone in the town survive?

A few days later, Mother stood with the crowd around the Western Town Gate. They were waiting for the Chinese soldiers who were expected to make a grand entrance. Firecrackers exploded; people cheered. A colorful silk dragon snaked through the streets to the beat of drums and horns.

Wuhu was an ancient town built in the Han Dynasty, two hundred years before Christ. The narrow and curved back alleys were paved in cobblestones and lined with red brick walls. Behind the walls, square houses with round full moon doors and carved wooden window shudders encircled courtyards. Tall barricades surrounded the town, with huge wooden gates carved in the pattern of a dragon spitting fire. Each gate sat in the direction of north, east, south and west.

The gate slowly opened. Mother wept for joy. She was expecting a far distant cousin by marriage to come home. In her fantasy, she saw a heroic prince riding a white horse entering her heart.

Mother had met her cousin Ming, my father to be, when her aunt married his uncle. Lin was seven years old and Ming was twelve. Lin was the prettiest little girl in town with her huge eyes and buster brown haircut. Ming was a glamorous little boy with five servants waiting on him hand and foot. She remembered vividly the day they met. Ming held court with other children from the neighborhood. He was telling a far-fetched fairy tale, to impress the little cousin from the Wang family. Mother said she knew her destiny was to marry her cousin.

A year passed, Mother went to Nanjing to attend Teacher's College. Father was also in Nanjing working in the Educational Department under his uncle, teaching Economics. Mother did poorly in academic studies. She had dreamed of becoming an artist. But her parents would not give permission. Girls who study art are loose women and whores, they would say. Father encouraged her to take Chinese painting lessons. He admired Mother's talents.

Nanjing was the Capital City when Chiang Kai-shek was in power. Nanjing streets were broad and clean, lined with green tropical palm trees. The buildings were Western style two or three stories high. Mother loved to see her reflection in the clear glass when she passed the doors along the streets. There were parks, cafes and store windows. Here she rekindled her relationship with Father. They went to the movies, ballroom dancing halls and European art galleries despite the turmoil around them. The Communist Revolution was everywhere. Each day, there were student demonstrations in Center Square of the city. Illegal posters, protesting Chiang Kai-shek's Party were pasted on the walls. Flags were waved and slogans were shouted. There were daily arrests and executions. Houses were set on fire; people were tied with their hands behind their backs, shot in the head, bodies were abandoned on the streets.

When Mother's parents heard of her friendship with father, they brought her home and locked her in her room. They had prearranged her marriage to a mayor's son from another town. Why? They did not like Ming's mother. She was mean, they said. Lin would have a mean mother-in-law, they said. So they were going to force her to marry someone else.

Mother's brother, Kang-Shing, an aunt and some of Father's friends arranged for Mother to flee from her parents' home. They secretly escorted her to the train station. On the train to Nanjing, Mother realized she was running away from an unreasonable past, toward an unknown future. A few months later, she married Father in Nanjing. None of her family attended the wedding.

Father grew up in the same Wuhu city in Anhui province as Mother did. He was born in 1921 when there were civil wars between warlords in China. Citizens lived in terror under the iron thumb of different tyrants. Rich and poor were set apart; girls and boys were sold and bought for a price of one meal; concubines and prostitutes, boy or girl, were used and discarded; opium dens were common and venereal diseases epidemic; Western imperialism coiled around China like a venomous serpent. The social system no longer worked; the older generation fought as hard as they could to hold onto their traditions while the younger ones were confused and lost in political battles. Life had pulled Chinese people in many directions.

Father came from a rich, aristocratic family, the Tsuai's. We were Han people. There had been many scholars, government officials and royal associates throughout generations during the Ming dynasty. After the Qing dynasty, Tsuai family had turned a rich merchant. Father would announce proudly he had five servants exclusively serving him when he was but five years old. However, he suffered from the failure of his parents' marriage. He was twenty years old when his father passed away from a reckless life-style. He had no choice but to care for his widowed mother for the next thirty-six years.

It was a Chinese tradition to name their children after a family genealogy. Every generation's middle name is prerecorded in the book. Father was given the name Tze-Chu, great horse in Chinese. His nickname is Ming; bright and clear like the sun, like the moon. He was the first-born son of the fourth generation in the Tsuai family. "Tze Dai Tong Tang" (Four generations live under one roof) they said. Everyone flattered him for being the important one who would inherit the Tsuai family land, properties, businesses and fortune. He was the richest among the rich in town. Then, with tears hidden, he confided he was really brought up by servants, and seldom saw his parents.

When Japan invaded China he was sent to Shanghai at the age of sixteen to live with his fourth aunt and uncle on his mother's side. The living situation did not work out. The Japanese soldiers occupied Shanghai. His aunt and uncle had already fled from their home on their way to Chunking, Sichuan with burdens of their own. Father found lonesome living in the family warehouse by himself. He took work in a bank managed by a distant relative. He was abandoned. No one cared for his well being or his education. His mother was busy gambling at the Mahjong table. His father was addicted to opium. With all the wealth promised to him, he cried every day. One day, a light of hope shone on his shadowed life. He met Mr. Doo, a fellow worker. Mr. Doo offered him a free education and a bright future, as long as Father followed his suggestions. Mr. Doo also introduced Father to an ideological utopia, which would certainly be the future China someday.

Father had found a meaning in life and he had a mission. There was so much corruption in the current government, with injustice of a ruling upper class and the repression of a working class. He would be able to make changes for a better world. He was enthusiastic. And he was in love.

Yee Mei was dark and slim with two thick long braids and a round moon face. She was one year younger than Father. She came from a peasant family who knew how to work with water buffaloes and donkeys. She had a theatrical voice and displayed dramatic talents. Yee Mei studied at the same college and shared many similar feelings and points of view with Father. Together, they would join the Long March. They would help make the red sun rise from the East.

Six years later, they became underground fighters, battling against both Japanese and Chinese Nationalist armies. Twelve young comrades traveled together, fueled by their revolutionary dreams. They performed as a political theater group.

Father's happiness was shattered when he was told Yee Mai was killed along with ten other friends, while he left the group to visit his mother. Sad news turned into a nightmare. Not only did he lose his closest friends, he was ordered to lie. His friends actually died in a battle against the Japanese troops; however, he was told to announce Chang Kai-shek's army caused the tragic event. Father could not follow the command. On the contrary, he decided to tell the truth. He firmly believed he was making the most appropriate decision.

Father stepped onto the wooden platform and started to tell his version of the story.

"Comrades! Comrades! If we truly believe in Marx's principles, we must face the truth ..." He started to see stars dancing. He was knocked unconscious. He never got the chance to make his speech.

When he woke up in the hospital with a concussion, he learned an unknown person had hit him over the head with a heavy broom behind his back. His father's younger brother went to visit him in the hospital and brought him home for healing. Father stayed with his uncle for the next three months. He reestablished family ties. His uncle also introduced him to other books, which held philosophies conflicting with Communist principles. For the first time, he read Dr. Sun Yet-sen's book, Three Principles of the People: of the People, for the People and by the People. He learned about Nationalism and Capitalism.

Years later, he would passionately discuss those principles in the bathroom when I was brushing my teeth, disregarding my request for privacy.

Two years before the war ended, Father withdrew from the Communist party and joined the Nationalist army. He continued to fight the Japanese war. He was made a captain when the war was over, but Father knew his war was over, too. He would have to flee for his life someday, somewhere.

One year after he married Mother, they fled Mainland China. On the way to Taiwan, he sat by Hong Kong Bay, burning page after page of the journals he kept during his years of revolution. I think by burning his journal, he burned away parts of his spirit and dreams. He was no longer an ambitious man. He was unable to produce a diploma to prove his education beyond the high school level, for he feared to be accused of being a spy. He worked in a shipping company as a clerk for the next fifteen years.

Sometimes, I wanted to shake him and ask him, where was the idealistic young man who wanted to change a five-thousand-year-old China? I was insensitive to a man who had had the strength to endure a difficult historical time.

Home for Father was a lost imperial China.

Besides Taiwan, two smaller islands, Jinmen and Matsu, stood along the west coast of Taiwan in the middle of the China Sea. The Taiwanese government used Jinmen and Matsu for their military bases. The Cold War had started. American navy ships circled around Jinmen and Matsu, acting as a big brother protecting Chiang Kai-shek's power. The American soldiers saturated Tein-Mu district in Taipei city, hanging out in bars and flirting with Suzy Wong bargirls and her world. Every other day, Communist China fired at the two little islands with their half-ass routine bombs, a disturbing echo. Were we ever to be free of war? The bombings eventually stopped during the Sixties; however, the threat continued. We became accustomed to the quivering fear of the ghostly shadow of a war beneath our feet.

Chang Kai-shek had sent a troop of ill organized, poorly disciplined army soldiers to receive Taiwan after the World War II. History was repeated: the soldiers raped and robbed. Once again, the Taiwanese people fought back. The battle day, 'February Eighteen' was said to turn the rivers red. After the Communist Revolution, Chiang Kai-shek moved his government to Taiwan. We lived under Martial Law. No one was allowed to speak Taiwanese in schools or public gatherings. No native Taiwanese held high positions. Most Taiwanese and Mandarins were segregated.

Every year, on October Tenth, we celebrated Independence Day when Chiang Kai-shek's Nationalist Party, led by Dr. Sun Yet-sen overthrew the Last Emperor. The previous evening, Mother would pack three lunch boxes, one canteen of water for Father. We set off for our journey to downtown Taipei, with blankets and sweaters. We joined the crowds on the pavement of the Presidential Square. Ping and I would fall asleep under a starry night amidst thousands of others. Father chatted easily with the people around us. At the break of dawn, we heard the roaring shake of the military tanks. People stood in silence. Father picked up Ping and held him over his shoulders. I stood a head shorter, watching the backs of somber figures. I felt buried under a mass of crows, dark and depressive. My heart was heavy, watching as best I could. The powerful military tanks zoomed through the trembling earth. It seemed to reflect the inner terror of war. I did not feel pride, but saddened. How fear could take over the human psyche. We begin to worship the very thing we are terrified of, like war.

After I enrolled in the junior high schools, I was not allowed to dress in anything but black and white or beige military uniforms. Boys wore military crew cuts. To rebel, they would grease their hair in heavy oil during the holidays. The girls had to chop their hair at ear level. We tried to sneak curves in our straight haircut. Frequently the curves met their fate under the teacher's cruel scissors. We sang military marching songs in public gatherings. We had riffle-shooting lessons once a month. Military police stood on the unpaved street corners. Jeeps and soldiers were everywhere.

The two worlds living so closely together would be divided by separate inner turmoil. Mandarin eyes were vacant with fear. Anger and resentment set in Taiwanese hearts spread through the thick air. Day in, day out, people expected the war to burst out again. The Korean War happened to the north in the Fifties. The Vietnam War happened to the south in the Sixties. The Chiang Kai-shek's army automatically drafted boys who did not go to colleges. Soldiers were sent to Jinmen and Matsu. They would be dust should a war happen between Mainland China and Taiwan. So enraged teenagers fought on the streets as gangsters. Or they became bookworms, burying themselves in the challenge of heavy examinations, hoping to avoid the military service by entering colleges and universities.

I would play in the schoolyard with the lizards and grasshoppers. I drew pictures of houses, but then the houses disappeared, the colors remained: black and red. A stonewall gleamed through the black. It was Ping's face carved on the wall. I was certain he was going to die on the battlefield.

The yearning to go 'home' towered over our panic of another imminent war. For decades this yearning for 'home' would fill the hearts and souls of the thousands of displaced Mandarins living in Taiwan. It would follow me all the way to America, invade my marriage and, for a while shatter my career.

Three

Grandma's generation of women sat and embroidered. They had their feet bound, and women were married off. She did not have her feet bound, but she lived in a tradition where women lacked free will. The marriage to Grandpa was disastrous.

We had an ancestor-alter in the corner of the dining area. Grandpa's picture was hung in the center. Grandma and Mother were moody. Whenever they were angry they would beat Ping and me. So I would kneel in front of Grandpa's picture. I prayed he would protect me from the miserable beatings I got. Grandma cursed Grandpa and me in the same fashion: we were both dead-slave ghosts. He had a round face and a broad smile. I had a round lovely face and a broad smile. He wore glasses and I was the only person nearsighted in our family. I secretly communicated with him in my heart.

Her temper drove everyone away. She could not see her own flaw. Throughout my entire childhood she repeatedly told me she wanted me to write a novel about her, except she did not realize her version of herself was not what I perceived. In her eyes she was the great beauty, the heroine, and the beloved one. To me, she stayed a witch.

The Tsuai family was not politically active like the Chai family was. The family owned half of Wuhu city business. There were four sons and nine daughters in the Tsuai family. My grandfather was the oldest. His second brother studied political science in Shanghai University. His third brother registered himself in a temple to be a Buddhist monk. The youngest son was a poet who died at the age of twenty-one, leaving his young bride a widow for the rest of her life. Mother Tsuai gave her daughters away except the youngest one who was two years older than my father.

Their marriage was truly a double happiness at the beginning. They were both young in their teens. One year later they produced a son, Ming Tsuai, my father. It was an extravagant, welcoming home. Shang Lang was so proud. She was the oldest daughter-in-law who gave a first-born boy to the fourth generation Tsuai clan. She came from a well-respected family. But something chewed her up inside. She did not sleep or eat well. One day, she sent word to her father's home. Soon her younger sisters were sent to help and keep her company.

My grandpa loved to sing Chinese opera. He was an aristocrat. He was not allowed to join an opera troop. So he bought a theater, an opera troop, cast himself as a leading female singer. On the opening night of his performances, Grandma marched onto stage and dragged him off. It was disgraceful, in her mind. A family man and an upper class master dressed like a woman, singing, dancing in public … He did not forgive her. He left home and disappeared for two years.

"If your grandpa had lived, he would be so proud to see you dance," Grandma spoke in her low throaty voice, flashing her yellowish teeth. A long strand of ash dangling from her cigarette butt made her finger nails smoky gray. She had become a chain smoker and a compulsive gambler. She frequently disappeared to the "Mahjong" table for three or four days without taking a break. She would carry a pot of tea and a bag of fried peanuts as she marched off to her destination with enthusiasm. She claimed her gambling habit was caused by her disastrous marriage.

"Your grandpa was such a good opera singer," Grandma shook her head. "He was a sculptor, too. He made enormous amount of masks and strange creatures. He stored them down in the basement. When we were young, being a sculptor was such a shameful thing. He could never take his sculptures out of his workshop and show anyone his work. It was a bad time, you know, we thought about things in different ways. We were aristocratic." Grandma spoke in her proud voice, making me believe she admired her late husband.

Along with the passion for opera, Grandpa had a few other obsessions. First he was addicted to opium. Later he kicked the opium habit, but took refuge in alcohol. Grandpa persisted in his visit to the red light district (prostitutes) until 1937 when the Japanese war broke out. He had passed syphilis to Grandma, causing an up-set within the family. Grandma asked for a divorce in vain. The marriage continued on again and off again. He died of liver failure at an early age. Before he died, he made Father promise to never leave my grandmother; thus my parents never stopped arguing. Grandma remained a tyrant of the family until her death in 1979.

My first memory of Grandma was during one of the typhoon in Keelun. Moments before I was asleep, in a flash of an eye I was sitting on a makeshift bed watching the whole scene. Time had come to a stop. There was no beginning and no end. Maybe a typhoon was hitting Taiwan, at the same time it also created a storm within Grandma.

The grayish wall by the bed where I slept with Grandma had a big hole, knocked in by the raging storm. Water poured in, trees swayed, the wind howled, uprooting everything in sight. But it was not the typhoon or even the cavity in the wall which frightened me. It was Grandma's scream. A witch was casting her spell, her dancing shadow moved in the dark. She made horrific shrieking sounds. At the age of three, I was being introduced to Grandma's world of sorrow. She would cry out her pain for me to witness.

Keelun was meant to be temporary. Grandma had said we would be able to have a good place to live because of her status. Her brother worked in Chiang Kai-shek's government as a high official. Nobody could beat that fact. We should kow-tow to her. However, when the typhoon hit Taiwan Grandma lost her temper and dignity. She turned into a dancing witch.

I became extremely curious about Grandma after the typhoon. In the morning I sat on a small bamboo stool peeking at her. She let her hair down and combed it with slow-motion easiness. I wondered why a witch cared so much about her hair? Thick clouds overshadowed the sky making the day gray and damp. Grandma sat on a sick yellowish bamboo stool in front of a sick yellowish bamboo vanity desk. Her image reflected through a long and narrow mirror. She was wearing a black and gray widow's Chungseng dress with Mandarin collar and Pan-Que buttons. Her hair, which she teased and combed with shimmering raven oil was black and gray with a few streaks of white here and there. That afternoon she combed it with a small wooden comb while humming a tune unfamiliar to my ears, an ancient tune with the Chinese opera flavor, a far away world, yet close by. A fox song? In the end, she tightened her grip on her hair to fashion a small bun behind her thin neck.

In my mind she was a witch, I could not admit she was beautiful. I was afraid of her. It seemed she let her hair down for two occasions: in the morning and when she became hysterical. Grandma wore no make up. She always wore black or dark gray, with a pair of black leather shoes and white socks.

After she finished her daily ritual of hair combing, she would look at the mirror, and then smile at me, "Si Yia Tao! Ken Zhe Muo ..." "Dead-slave girl! What are you looking at! You won't find anything good in my face!"

"Nai Nai! (Grandma) Can you comb my hair?" I would plead with her.

While I was pleading with Grandma, I imagined my dead Grandpa standing behind her. I looked at Grandpa's portrait as often as a refuge from the present moment. He would appear as she combed her hair, as she spoke to me, as she made pronouncements. Later my attachment and devotion to Grandpa would switch to the pigtailed Dorothy in the poster Father had given me.

"No! You're a yellowed hair (thin hair in Chinese expression) dead-slave girl! You've got no hair long enough to be combed. Go fetch me a glass of morning tea!"

Grandpa faded away. I ran to the kitchen. I called out to A-Mai, the woman who helped out when my parents were out.

"Take this glass of tea to Nai Nai. Be a good girl and don't drop the glass. This afternoon, I'll take you to the pond behind our house. I'll teach you how to climb a tree." A-Mai smiled warmly.

I'll be a good girl and not drop this glass of tea or I'll get beatings from both my mother and grandmother. My life isn't as valuable as this glass, which they treasure so much. I'll be careful.

A-Mai will teach me how to climb a tree. And then she will teach me how to catch the moon between my fingers in the dusk. We will hide the moon in my belly, where dreams will shine at night. Witches will turn into compassionate goddesses, who will teach me how to dance and fly.

I can be careful. I can be a good girl. Not a dead-slave girl.

I held the glass on my left palm. I secured it with my right thumb and middle finger. I handed the glass to Grandma. I saw my dead Grandpa smiling. She sipped her tea. She held the glass in her yellowish tobacco stained fingers.

"Little dead-slave girl! Look at the way you walk! You have the good luck to be born now. If you were born at my time, we would have to bind your feet. You could never walk the way you do. I was lucky, too. They were binding my feet in the backyard when I was seven years old. My mother and aunts and neighbor-hood women joined forces to break me down. I was so strong. I screamed so loud. My father heard me from the living room across the house. Father was a revolutionist and he was mad. He came to my rescue. He told the whole house-hold there would be no more bound-feet in his house. You should see everyone's face. I laughed. I couldn't stop laughing until my mother slapped my face. But I couldn't get out of the web of Chinese woman's fate; I married your grandpa and lived a miserable existence. We Chinese women live in shadows. We live under-ground. Perhaps someday I will tell you my story and you can write a novel about me." She talked loud and blunt, except when the subject was her husband who died at the age of thirty-nine.

Although the daughter-in-law traditionally was meant to serve the husband's mother, for me it was another euphemism for 'slave girl'. As has been noted, 'If not a wife or a slave we could have been swordswomen and avenge our families.' At the time I was not possessed with such warriorship. I wished to be as strong as

Grandma. If I could awaken Grandpa from the dead, maybe I could ask him to stop the beatings in my household?

◆   ◆   ◆

Just when Grandma was born China was about to make a change, not knowing how or what direction. Rich men inherited houses, land, business and servants. They wore round honeydew shaped hats over their pigtails, long silk robes with short rayon jackets. They indulged in opium, played cicadas fighting games, and held birdcages in their hands. They could have many concubines. Occasionally, they took boy and girl servants for their pleasures. They were able to discard anyone who displeased them. Rich women were married off. They stayed home to sew and embroider as their feet were bound. Most of them considered themselves lucky to be the first wives. However, when they grew old and undesirable their husbands took in many young concubines. The first wives often won bad reputations by murdering baby boys born by the second, third or fourth concubines, fearing they would lose the inheritance. The women who were bound within the same household were jealous of each other. Despair and torment lasted life long. Poor people did not exist in the eyes of the rich, except to be used as doormats.

Grandma's father was a revolutionist hero with Dr. Sun Yet-sen. He tried to make a difference. He wanted social reform. He began to wear western style suits, had his boys cut off their pigtails and had them sent to America to study the modern world. He rescued Grandma from bound-feet; yet, when it came to his daughter's marriage he firmly indicated Grandma should follow the tradition. She should swallow her pride, submit to her fate.

In 1911, China overthrew the royal Qing Dynasty but the power fell into the hands of warlords. The country was divided, citizens lived under tyrannical terror. It took fifteen years of civil war to unify China. By then, Shang Lang was twenty-three years old. She had lived through two civil wars. She had a son, my father. She was at personal war at home with her husband, my grandfather.

Previously, the Boxer Rebellion and the Opium War had wiped out an entire generation of middle and upper class. The Japanese war (Second World War) destroyed what was left in China. During the Japanese war, Shang Lang went to a remote farmland owned by Grandpa's family. There she killed pigs and chickens to feed the peasants, and then she demanded rent from the farmers. She took care of her two sisters, organizing their wedding ceremonies in the midst of war and famine. She stayed with her father and his concubine until his last breath while they traveled through the mountains. She conducted his funeral with no tears and no smile. She showed up at her son's doorstep when she sensed he was in danger, possibly being arrested by a Japanese secret agent. She helped my father to escape. Sadly, she had had to bury Grandpa who died during the war.

Whenever Mother complained about living with Grandma, Father said, "I promised papa I wouldn't leave her."

"Never mind if she beat our daughter to death?"

Chinese have ways of beating their children along with the cursing words. Harsh words strung like bad pearls replay themselves from time to time.

"Dead-slave girl! You deserve to die. You want to die! Worthless piece of meat! Go and die! Leave me in peace! I must owe you a death in my previous live! Even after you die, cow head and horse face ghosts and monsters will devour you! You are the garbage picked out by the misfortunate fate! Worthless slave girl head!"

Words rained on us along with bamboo sticks, feather dusters and the soles of shoes. Grandma's favorites would be knocking our heads with her finger knuckles, twisting our earlobes till our faces turned red, digging her fingernails into the skin on our thighs. Most time, death was the weapon.

"I deserve to die! Let death fall upon me!" Father hit himself across the face, pleading with Mother.

"But your father left her himself!" Mother screamed.

"I couldn't leave her. I can't leave her now. Thunder will strike me twice if I break my promise!" Father said.

"You spineless worm! You do deserve to kneel in front of your mother with the night potty on your head!" Mother cursed.

What could he say between my mother and his mother? At the very end of Grandma's life Mother was her sole caretaker. She bathed her corpse. Carefully dressed her in a traditionally white silk Chungseng dress and an elaborate white silk headband embroidered with pearls, jade and rubies. She combed her hair with fragrant oil and rubbed rose water into her nose and ears. Mother placed a pair of white silk shoes shaped like boats on her feet, so she could ride across the river between life and death. She dabbed bright red lipsticks on Grandma's lips, placing a jade cicada inside her mouth. All the time she continued to complain about Grandma as if nothing had happened.

I had a dream. Grandma appeared. Her luscious body shone through her sky blue flowing chiffon dress, half naked. Her raven black hair was flying behind her waist. She was dancing. Her arms waved in circular motion. Scenes of old China shimmered behind her. Worn out wooden houses painted imperial green and red. Carved dragons and lions roared on the stone rooftops. Behind the rice paddy landscape, a pagoda temple glimmering through layers of clouds atop of a purple mountain. Under the mountain a single golden boat floated across the gushing river. She called out our ancestors, earth gods and foxes. We danced in a ritualistic circle up and down hills. She made a circling gesture, pointing her index finger towards me. I reappeared in a cluttered high tech room. There were dishwashers, television sets, and flying cars. I squeezed myself past a thin wall breaking out of the claustrophobic room. I ran over a meadow in slow motion. Grandma ran towards me from the opposite direction. She was bouncing a giant pink balloon. She whispered in my ears and sang softly of fox songs. The pink balloon floated above our heads. We laughed all the way to eternity.

◆   ◆   ◆

I attended an all female junior-high school. The class began at five o'clock in the afternoon and ended around ten at night. There was not enough school space to accommodate the number of students who needed schooling in the early Sixties in Taiwan. Most children who received mediocre scores in their elementary sixth grade tests were sent to the night shifts. I belonged to the mediocre group. We were ages thirteen to fifteen, wearing the same uniforms.

The school was located on the outskirts of Taipei City. The old Japanese style building was deteriorating. The pine wood paneled walls, combined with the claustrophobic low ceilings created an unrelenting somber atmosphere. One light bulb hung in the ceiling; otherwise the room was dim. Tiers of hills surrounded the school grounds. Pale grayish-green rice paddies. They rolled down the slopes. A large bamboo forest extending from the edge of the rice paddies suggested a forbidden dream, a secret wish hidden in the cave of the heart. The moonlit atmosphere was funereal evoking the fear of the unknown.

Whenever a history class about five thousand years of facts and historical names was about to begin, I would gaze out the classroom windows, where the mysterious shadows of the bamboo forest danced in moonlight. Was there a fox in those dark woods? Or a ghost? Or fairies? My mind would wander to old China, to my ancestors, to the fox myth and ghost stories told by my father. How the female soprano in Chinese opera, played by a man, often belted out fox songs.

For thousands of years, the peasants in China worshipped the fox. Some depicted them as evil spirits while others appreciated their supernatural powers. Fox shrines were set up everywhere in China, deep in the rural farmland, along with the Taoist earth gods and ancestors.

My great great grandparents had moved to a huge old farmhouse in Wuhu city from Tai Ping Village. As was their ancestors' custom, my parents told me they worshipped the fox. They had set up a fox shrine, decorated with flowers, fruits and nuts.

"Fox were vicious," Father's voice rang in my head, a singsong tune while the history teacher went on with her blah-blahs.

"Fox must come and feast. If they are neglected, the house can catch fire." When I listened to Father's tales, I thought how could a fox come to our house? People compacted their living quarters on top of each other in Taipei City. There was simply no room for a fox.

Mother inserted her opinion, "No. I disagree. Fox are gentle and kind spirits. People make shrines because fox are sacred. They save the people," she would tell her side of the story: one day, a fox came and waved its paws at her grandma who followed the fox, in spite of her fear, only to discover her house was on fire. She had enough time to call for help. Fox were spirits. They could predict things and help people avoid disasters.

The history teacher continued to emphasize how important it was for us to memorize China's historical past. My eyelids would fall with the heaviness of being Chinese and the importance of China's importance to be the center of the universe. I laughed. The name `China` in Chinese means the `center of the universe`. The history teacher took the meaning literally.

Grandma told a story of three wise men with long white beards. During the Tai Ping Tian Guo Rebellions in the Late Qing dynasty in 1900's, a group of bandits let their hair down to ride on their horsebacks. They ransacked the village in the name of "revolution". The bandits were called "Chang-Moa" (Chang-Moa means long hair). They entered her village, and then demanded all young men should be drafted. Soon, three old men appeared in the family courtyard. They came from nowhere and knelt in front of the leader of the Chang-Moa. Instantly, he changed his mind and left, without taking anyone with them. Grandma explained the old men had actually been foxes. Thus her family bowed to the image of the fox every morning.

I stared at the fat history book filled with printed lines of black square words. They made me think of ants crawling in my brain. I was supposed to finish reading the fifth chapter. I closed my eyes slightly, yearning to see a fox running free in the bamboo woods, singing.

"Dada (father) had said fox aren't animals. They're spirits." Mother's words danced in my half sleepy head, "that's why the fox stories we see in movies and read about in books aren't superstitions. They are very very real. The family is tied to the land. The land is tied to the spirit. We must go back to China. China is a magic place, where fox, ghosts and ancestors live among people. Not like Taiwan where everything is so empty and plain. Taiwan has no color, but China is different. We could walk to any remote place in China and suddenly the place would become a magic realm. Foxes can transform into human beings and ghosts may trick our sense of reality. Taiwan is so dull and boring!"

Contemporary China, which I knew nothing about, was portrayed so much better, so superior. The moon was brighter; the cakes were sweeter; the trees were taller. The dragon lanterns during the lantern festival were much fiercer, with actual fire puffing from their mouths ... Meanwhile the Taiwanese government drew dreary images of Mainland China, with its people starving and surviving on tree barks and banana peels. The ugly Communist party members wore oxen heads and horse faces. Human skulls scattered on a deserted land.

As children, our parents, relatives and teachers taught us we were Mandarins. Again and again, they saturated us with our ancestors, ghost stories, fox tales and the concept of how great China was.

I learned why fox was not included in our Lunar Zodiac Calendar of twelve animals, which represented the years: In our society fox was supernatural, all knowing.

In ancient times scholars prepared for public examination to further their careers by isolating themselves in temples and gardens to study. During these retreats they experienced many strange thoughts, perhaps due to frequent tales. Foxes, Fairies, Ghosts, Supernatural Phenomena would emerge from their minds. In our family the fox was respected as supernatural—after all fox had showed up in the first known folktale as a mystical animal who clothed an abandoned blind prince.

Grandma lived among her Feng Shui rituals, family predecessors, spirits, and earthly gods. She sang soft fox songs in her low and breathless whispering voice. Father loved to talk loudly about fox during the mealtime. Most stories happened to him personally.

"Before the Revolution, I lived in this magnificent house in Shanghai," he would begin with a grand gesture, "it was a family house belonging to our ancestors, the Tsuai family. But it's deserted when I lived there. My best friend Ku was living with me. We were young students fighting the Japanese War. We stayed in that house with a few belongings. It became notably noisy at night right up above where we were sleeping. We knew there were fox living in the attic. We tried to avoid them, but we were tired and grumpy. After a few nights of restless sleep, Ku became quite upset. He started to pick up a broom and hit the ceiling with his broomstick. The fox didn't back off. They stomped and tramped and made more noise. I begged Ku to stop. He wouldn't. His eyes bulged out and his face reddened. He said he didn't believe fox could have psychic powers. So Ku hit the ceiling a little louder and the fox responded with equal vigorous energy. Finally the fox stopped. I slept beautifully that night. When I woke up I noticed Ku was gone. I crossed the moon door (a Chinese full moon shaped garden door) and entered into the courtyard. Guess what? I found Ku sleeping like a baby under a tree, completely naked. Apparently, the fox stripped him and brought him outdoors while he was sound asleep."

Why did mysteries never happen to me? I could do nothing but dance and memorize the boring textbooks. Even though I studied hard the tedious details of those textbooks I could not help but close my eyes and let my head drop onto my folding arms. Half-sleeping, and half-dreaming, I would reconstruct Father's excited voice.

"I was walking along the abandoned mountain road with my friend Liang. We were trapped in Yellow Mountain for three months and we were wrecked. For days we walked through woods without seeing a ghost. Japanese were fighting with Chinese; Communists were fighting with Nationalists; and we were fighting with everyone, or rather we were trying to escape from anyone who would catch us and draft us into their armies or shoot us on the spot. We were students with no school to go to and we were civilians, acting like soldiers with no weapons to defend ourselves. We were about twenty years old and perfect targets as suspects for any army that came across our path. Liang was running a fever and I was throwing up from hunger. Then, we saw this hut. We crawled into the hut on all fours and lay down with exhaustion." Father had a way being dramatic and effective when he told stories.

"I was dozing off that night. A tiny peasant woman with a pair of bound-feet walked in the hut. She put some food and water by the door, and then she walked around the room with her crippled diminutive feet. I was terrified. The oddness of this woman made me freeze. I wanted to wake Liang up, but I couldn't move. Finally, she walked towards me and stopped right by my feet. I lay there stiff without a breath staring at her hovering over me," Father would stop; he wanted to make sure everyone was listening.

"She wasn't a human being. She was a fox dressed up as a peasant. She had a printed blue flower jacket on over a pair of black cotton pants, a blue bandanna was wrapped around her head. She looked at me intensely for a moment. Then she turned slowly away and disappeared with her wobbly steps. I was unable to stir. I don't think we would have survived without the food and water she left by the door."

These stories were sharp contrast to the reality of my parents struggle but I would come to realize they helped make their survival possible.

At those times I wished I were in China living my parents' lives. At the same time, deep down I yearned to belong to the heart of Taiwan where I grew up, where I did not see any fox. I was torn apart by the conflicting feelings. I wanted to know where I belonged. Ha! A fox with her crippled diminutive feet acted like a traditional Chinese woman of my grandma's generation. I thought of my feet. How I cringed when I had to put on a pair of new shoes. Fox sang songs of mystery; women sang songs of misery.

What will be my song?

◆   ◆   ◆

There were always dreams/
Amazing queer dreams/
Penetrating my psychic world, night after night/
Beautiful lovely and sentimental dreams/
In those dreams I danced out stories of my life/
In those dreams I danced/

In those dreams I leapt, a ballet grand jete/
Up onto a lofty circular lotus petal/
Up towards light/
Then down into a long dark hole/
Falling/
In those dreams I saw a courageous future/
Weaved by some odd mathematic patterns/
Unknown/

There were colors everywhere/
I struggled through layers of grey/
At the end there was a rainbow/
Blue bird fly/

I was animated, lively/
I could swim/

I could run/
I could soar/
Meditating in a pile of old spinning musical records/
Mozart, Bach, Stravinsky/

In my dreams I shrank smaller and smaller/
Dreams would dictate/
I stepped aside/
Watching the drama of life stories play/

In my dreams I was the audience/
Looking at the gigantic movie screen/
I curled up watching/
Life frolicking/

There were conflicts in my dreams/
Which way should I go?/
Ballet? Jazz? Folk Songs? Modern Dance?/

Out of the corner of my eyes/
I saw boys jumping in my dreams/
Boys wearing white sneakers/
All that Jazz/
I indulgently danced/
All that Jazz/
I danced around my dreams/

In those dreams there were boys all over/
Dominating me/
Leading me/
Accompanying me/

In those dreams I was entrapped/
Striving to break through a cocoon/
I was terrified/
Shivering/

In those dreams I struggled/

Entrapped in a pine coffin/
I was anxious/
Gulping for breath/
Boys wore masks/
Dominating me yet unreachable/

In those dreams I struggled/
Pushing through layers of red/
Cracking through the coffin/
Breaking through the cocoon/
Free/
Free of boys' domination/
I leapt across the horizon/
I twirled and twirled/
Freedom was the movement in my dreams/

◆   ◆   ◆

I stayed at junior high for three years, dreaming. Each year, I grew up a little, gradually turning from a child to a young woman. School never interested me. The studies rigid and formulaic.

There was a boy's school in the same district across the rice field. The boys would clutter in groups on the street corners, waiting for the same buses every night. While we girls joined hands to walk towards the bus stops, we had moments of thrill. We could smell them miles away. Boys looked at us with their cocky smiles. They wore their military hats low, tilted to one side like the American cowboys in movies. Some of them smoked in a seductive manner. They changed the chemistry in the air, perfuming the streets with their boys' odors.

Whenever we passed them we tingled. Smiling widely we swayed our hips, we stuffed handkerchiefs inside our undershirts, pushed our chests forward.

One night, a boy walked slowly towards me. He reached into his pocket and handed me a letter. I took the letter, pretending I really did not see him.

At home in my bedroom I was in a cold sweat. Imagine a boy gave me a letter? Someone would be brave enough to give me a note. I went to sleep without knowing the letter's content. I did not dare to open the letter.

The letter safely pocketed in my shirt lay untouched for days, there for me to treasure. A week went by, then a month. I was possessed by an unopened letter.

Two months later the boy approached me again. I was walking on a narrow path near the rice field. Rice shoots were sprouting in the brisk, spring afternoon. Wind blew softly, brushing against my ears.

Did I hear a sexy fox song near by? I lowered my head, unable to look at him. Did I read his letter? I could not make a sound. He asked me to the movies Saturday afternoon. I said nothing. He said he would wait for me by the cinema.

On Saturday morning, I opened his letter. He expressed his admiration for me. He loved my dancing on television. I looked pretty and so tall on screen. Did I have many boyfriends? Would he have a chance to be my boyfriend? I folded the letter into a tiny square and gingerly placed it back in my shirt pocket.

Noon came and went. I had lunch with Mother and Ping. They wanted me to go with them to visit our granduncle and aunt. I told them I had a lot of homework to do. I locked myself in front of my study desk. My eyes were fixed on one spot. The Judy Garland poster. Finally, I got up and stood in front of a narrow mirror mounted on the wall. I was home but I did not have a Toto or any friends. I was alone. In my imagination 'Dorothy' was a close friend, someone who would understand my pent up feelings. What it was to be a suffering human being, not an idol. Years later I would learn how wrong I had been. Judy Garland loved her stardom.

It was two o'clock now. The movie would start any minute. The boy would be standing by the gate waiting. I began to gradually peel off my clothes. One by one until I was stark naked in front of the mirror. I imagined the boy standing next to me kissing my neck, my breasts, my back and my mouth. Warmth surged through my body.

As I stood there I thought what does he actually know about me? Did he understand mother spent two hours making me up before I appeared on television? Did he see the invisible rope my parents tied me with? Maybe I would have gone to the movie if he had not mentioned my dancing image on the TV screen. What I saw in the mirror was a midget. My face was round. My nose flat. My jaw too square. I had no nose bridge. My eyebrows did not really have the thick arches mother created each time I performed. They told me I was as beautiful as Elizabeth Taylor. Mother and Father wanted me to have a cosmetic surgery. They wanted my eyes slit open to form double lines. They would love to make my nose bridge long and pointed. They would like to shave down and narrow my jaw, implant breasts, thicken my hair. They would like me to be tall.

I was told to lie about my age. They insisted I could be born in 1949. 'I was too short to be born in 1948.' I had to be one year younger to fit my height. I started to see the words "short and ugly" shimmering over the number "48" and "tall and beautiful" over "49". I wondered if they ever considered my height when I was neglected and starving. Everything about me was petite. I thought of the boy. He would not like me when he found out how short and boring I really was. I did not have much to talk about either. A vast emptiness lived in my head. I had no intellectual smarts. Why would he be interested in me? Because I danced on TV? Did he know I was merely a puppet? Would he like to kiss a puppet? Father talked about how a dancer should not expect to get married, have children and live a normal family. Mother talked about how in this universe there was no boy good enough for me, perhaps a few rich ones. My parents were incapable of understanding me.

Clearly, the boy was in love with my image on television. I continued to dance in front of the mirror, imagining warm embraces and sensual kisses. He became as much a fantasy for me as I had been for him.

One Monday afternoon I saw him by the bus stop. He lowered his hat to salute me. Why I could not stop and talk to him? I wanted to tell him I had a thousand faces. That I was not too proud of the one he fell in love with. In any case he would have to go to my home and deal with my parents. I was blushing, my face aflame. What if I were free? Could I let go? Could I be held and kissed like the American boys and girls in the movies? Instead, I walked by in silence, feeling ashamed of my thoughts.

Throughout my childhood I would fabricate love stories, an Arabian Prince, a Tartar Warrior, a Japanese Samurai, an American Indian Chief or a Cowboy from the Wild West. They would come to rescue me, pull me from a dreary life usually I was whisked onto a moving train where I would be taken to an Oz, blooming with flowers and trickling water fountains. But the heroes would always betray me, leaving me to die alone where ghosts and monsters ate me up alive.

◆　　　◆　　　◆

Dear Diary:

The sky is clouded the earth muddy. Above me there are Papa, Mama and Grandma, besides me brother Ping. Why am I feeling so alone? I pray. There must be a God who can hear my calling. Please help me, God. Please enlighten me. Who am I? Why am I here? What position should I be on this earth? I see very little, my body, my surrounding, and my two feet above the ground, and they are small. I am not who Papa thinks. I am not the role Mama wants me to play. I do not exist in Grandma's eyes, except her little slave girl tagging along her, annoying her. Ping suffers more than I do, reacts to people, takes things harder. Who am I? God, can you hear me? I am calling you. My plea weighs a thousand pounds. God, I am not worthy. But I yearn to find the key that will unlock my heart. I will dive into the Pacific Ocean for that key.

Four

Father cherished his ivory chopsticks. They were off white, the tips were sharply pointed like Father's chin, their heads thick and round. The fine carved images along the sides reflected Father's well-defined "five Hats" (eye brows, eyes, nose, ears and mouth). A scholar's face, Grandma used to say. Ivory chopsticks were for honored scholars.

The two sticks one holds between the fingers and the palm in the restaurants are generally made of plain wood. However, the chopsticks in the home tell the tale of the user.

Since the first emperor, Chin Shi Huang, united the kingdoms and unified the culture twenty five hundred years ago Chinese people have lived under the iron thumb of ruling dictators. To make up for lack of power in national affairs, we have turned to eating. Food can no longer serve as a means to fulfill the hunger, it has to be more. And the tools for eating, chopsticks and bowls became the symbols of status.

The expression "Golden Bowl" means a high paying job, "Iron Bowl" a government job. When one receives an "Iron Bowl", his job should last forever unless there is a revolution, wherein one loses his "Iron Bowl" and his head at the same time. There are "Mongolian Chopstick Dance' and "Meao Tribal Wine Cup Dance" in Chinese folk dances to celebrate the well beings of minority people.

Mother had silver ones which she polished to a high sheen. She stored her silver chopsticks in a silk padded silver box. Only royal princesses used silver chopsticks. Mother told us in olden days the royal families feared for their lives. They were afraid of being poisoned and silver were used to detect the poison.

Grandma chose porcelain for her chopsticks. She wore colorless widow garb but her chopsticks were bright, colorful designs. Ping was given a pair of ebony square chopsticks for his hard stubborn clumsy right hand. Grandma indicated ebony was hard to break. I was given colorful lacquered wood. I often asked for the silver ones like Mother's, but I was informed I was not worthy of the silver.

When I turned sixteen I decided to change my utensils to the Western stainless steel fork and knife. Grandma popped her eyes and Father shook his head.

Mother laughed and used the fork and knife when we ate together. We used to pretend we were Elizabeth Taylor and Judy Garland during the mealtime. We escaped to Hollywood. We would beat the Chinese women's fate of being small and powerless.

As a matriarchal family Grandma's mood dominated us. Mother suffered under the nailing thumb of her mother-in-law. She was introverted and withdrawn. Naturally, her attention focused on her children. Ping held her heart while Father had escaped into Teacher Li's dance school in the hope of making me a star, meanwhile Mother was obsessed with Ping. Everyday she wandered along the alleys looking for Ping.

Before Ping's painful and aggravating involvement with street gangs (which eventually led to his arrest) I heard Mother's story about a street fight which she was later to feel was an omen of things to come.

She said, "I was sitting by the road on a bench against a wooden table in an illegal food stall. You should see the looks on the cook and his wife. They were standing eyes wide open ready to take off if there were any sign of police." Mother laughed. Squinting her eyes and thrusting her chin forward, she tilted her body side to side, giggling like a little child.

"I bring my own chopsticks, you know, you have to be careful about hepatitis these days. It's so dirty," She sighed dramatically, "but the Tofu dish was delicious! I was hungry and tired after working a whole day for uncle Hoo. It's my 'taomei' (upside down fungus ill fate) Everyday uncle Hoo goes home in his luxurious limousine and he doesn't even give me a lift. I don't exist but as a servant.

"How I wish I could really go home, back to Mainland China, maybe next year. Even rice tastes sweeter in Mainland China. I'm sick of working all day and cooking all night. Why can't your grandma help a little? She spends the entire day at a gambling table.

"It's my treat for my day. It costs me two pennies. While I was eating my beloved ill smelly fried Tofu dipped in a delicious chili sauce ..." she smacked her lips.

"I heard a great uproar. I saw a boy running past the food stall, raising a cloud of dust behind him. I soon saw three or four more boys holding knives and sticks, running after the boy. My heart jumped for a second. I thought he was Ping. Fortunately he wasn't. But he looked like Ping. I was confused.

"Then I heard the food stall cook swear in Taiwanese, 'Motherfucker those boys! Motherfucker the government and Chiang Kai-shek's crowd!' I paid up. How I wanted to finish my Tofu."

I knew better to question Mother's logic.

I starred in a weekly television show in Taipei. I performed at concerts and functions. Father successfully established the dance school and dance company for me. He continued to pull the strings dictating every detail of my life. Mother played a supporting role for the dynamic of a family centered on "Yung Yung's dance career", Ping faded further into the background.

Soon everyday Ping came home with a swollen face, bloody nose, bruised arms and legs, and torn clothes. His watch was stolen. His bicycle was gone. He lost his school bags. He was a wreck. No one but Mother paid any attention. She did not know how to handle my brother's anger. Ping denied he was involved with the Bamboo Gang. Who knows the truth?" Mother would push her lips forward, rolled her eyes upright and postured herself with dignity.

As it turned out it was in the Bamboo Forest at the end of the Bamboo Lane where they initiated their gang members and performed rituals. They were Mandarin kids, and most of them were children who grew up in army barracks and government settlements. They carried the myth and traditions of gangs from ancient China. They called themselves "Tai-Po," which came from the name of "Thirteen Tai-Po" connected to the Tang Dynasty, during the sixth century. "Thirteen Tai-Po" were folk heroes who practiced Martial arts to fight off warlords, bandits, and the oppressors of the people. Like Robin Hood, they took from the rich gave to the poor. They became legends, especially in the memories of Taiwanese soldiers who felt shamed by their own defeat. The soldiers passed on their folktales of "Thirteen Tai-Po" to their offspring. Their young ones tried to live up to the legend. So, hidden deep within the bamboo forest, the Bamboo Gang members slit their wrists and drew their blood offering their lives to their ancestral idols. Deep down in their hearts, they were frightened kids without motivation. They were living in a hostile environment. I knew it was not just the battles between Mandarins and Taiwanese, but also the daily abuse the boys faced within the walls of their own families and schools.

Mother gave birth to our youngest brother, AnAn. She was near forty when AnAn came full blast into this world with the energy of a storm. He cried loudly in the nursery room after his delivery. Father announced, "Kang Lin, we're having a strong son. Listen to his cries, loud and clear as if he were going to be a king. He is so strong. He'll be able to conquer the world for us. When he grows up, I'll send him back to Mainland China and he'll be able to recover our house for us."

So, they named him AnAn, Safeness or Protection. AnAn became the center of attention. I took upon the job of bathing him, changing the diapers and feeding him bottles during the night. Ping retreated to the streets this time without a mother chasing after him. Father stayed at home pondering our future. AnAn who at first seemed unconquerable became ill.

AnAn remained in the hospital for one month, hanging on. Eventually he recovered from his illness. Ping continued to look like a wounded soldier, however, no one paid attention to him. I continued to perform on television. Father was desperate. He would call out, "Kang Lin. Life isn't worth living. We've waited so long to go home. But where are we going? Nowhere! Yung Yung and Ping are teenagers now they will be able to take care of themselves. We could take rat poison. AnAn will go with us.

"Kang Lin! Look at the Dan-Shui River! It reminds me of the Yangtze River flowing across Wuhu city where I watched the boats sail by. It was so peaceful. Remember the time we were young and carefree? Who would guess we would have the Japanese war? Who would guess we would have the Communist Revolution? If we jump in the river the flowing water will carry us back home …

"Kang Lin! Should we pull the spirits of the hanging ghosts out of our spleen? Then we would be brave enough to hang ourselves and die as the hanging ghosts. Why should we keep going in Life? We are over forty years old now. Why do we need to hang on Life? Papa died when he was thirty nine." He said this as though Grandfather had received a great award.

Minute by minute, AnAn kept growing bigger and stronger. By the time he was one year old, he was able to climb the top of a wardrobe where he sat like the Monkey King. Mother yelled and screamed but could not catch up with his movements.

It was unbearable to hear them, Father's grim solution: We could all jump into the Dan-Shui River, or hang ourselves together in our bathroom, or take poison pills.

I retreated to the dance studio. Ping escaped to the bamboo woods and the riverbank where trees were green and water was blue. The gang would sit and talk, momentarily without worry. Friends like Cheng Duck, Wu Lizard, and Din Hunchback would ride their bicycles through the woods and play devil dares for a good show. Ping, the Tsuai Dog, inhaled his cigarettes and laughed hard, forgetting the dark shadows beyond the bamboo forest.

However, daily fights occurred when they confronted the 'Stream Gang' whose members were Taiwanese boys. Mother was called in by the school principle for conferences. Neighbors complained about the boy's behavior. Mother was puzzled, but she denied the possible trouble in her son's life.

It went on for three years. Then the police showed up at home to arrest Ping. They handcuffed him and took him off to the police station. This took my parents mind off group suicide. Chen Chin Shui, the head of the Stream gang was lying on a hospital bed in critical condition with multiple Samurai Sword slashes.

Ping's trial took place in the Taipei courthouse; we held our hearts by our throats waiting. Mother and I sat on a bench on the left side of the room, while Father was in the back with Mr. Wang, the lawyer. Ping was charged with assault along with four other boys. Nervousness and tension stretched out in the fabric of the space. No one talked.

We stood up when a small man wearing a black robe appeared. I recognized him to be the Judge, Mr. Lee. I had visited him at his home with Mr. Wang two days before the trial. He hammered the gavel. We sat down.

Then, five boys were brought in chained together. Their hands and feet were bound with heavy metal, making clacking sounds. The sight of Ping being chained like an animal nauseated me. I felt Mother's hand reach out and clutch me. Her hand was icy cold. I clenched my teeth and lips. No one cried.

Time dragged. The Judge was talking. The boys mumbled their answers.

"All convicted without bail!" the Judge yelled out loudly. The room became a compact box of turmoil. Shouting sounds resonated. Time was somersaulting. Ping turned his face. He looked at Mother.

His eyes enlarged, shocked with pain. Ping's jaw dropped open but no sound came out. His face turned green; his life was drained right out of him. He was wearing his beige high school uniform, but he looked more like a captured slave.

Mother stood up and leaned over. She could not reach out fully to touch Ping. Time slowed down, pressing and gliding in a holographic image. I tried to reach out too. I found my hands stretching, not knowing whom to grab. People were shouting and yelling. I heard voices everywhere but silence took command within, singled out my brother's turning face, Mother's leaning torso and my out stretched arms, which danced like howling wolves. Tears streamed down my cheeks. My eyes were there to witness the capture of my brother and the shuddering of my mother's soul.

My parents and I had no knowledge of what really happened. Ping alone knew the truth. The police came one morning. They handcuffed Ping. We were told Ping had stabbed the leader of an opposite gang. Days after Ping was taken away my parents and I were on the run. We were in the police station, the lawyer's office and the Judge's home trying to save Ping from being convicted.

I ran outside to look for a friend of mine. I asked him to take me on his motorcycle to see my college professor, Mr. Wang, who was also a lawyer. Mr. Wang made some arrangements. That night, he accompanied me to a ballroom dancing hall. Dancing cheek to cheek with the district attorney Mr. Ma, I begged for my brother's life. The dancing hall was a disguise. Mr. Ma, Mr. Wang and I were negotiating for Ping's life.

Mother was very quiet. Sometimes, she sat in front of the window, murmuring …"What did I do wrong … What did I do wrong …?" I locked myself inside of my room. I started to drink. First, it was red wine in the refrigerator, then it was whiskey in the curio cabinet, and finally I took the cooking wine from the kitchen. Now Mother had two troubled children. One was my brother sitting in jail. The other one was her daughter who was drunk every night.

The previous day, Mr. Wang and I went to the Judge Lee's house. We sat there drinking tea and making small stupid jokes. Mr. Wang pushed a red envelope enclosing a stack of money across the table. Things felt lighter with the money unloaded from our hands. The judge accepted the envelope, and walked away in his honored black robe. I looked for him. He was walking away down the hallway. No! I left Mother trembling behind. I chased after him. No! Stop! No! Judge! Please, I beg you. Please let my brother go! Please have Pity! Please! You are punishing my mother. I won't let you kill my mother. Looking at the Judge's tightened lips and empty eyes chilled my spine. I kept on pleading with him.

That afternoon the police called home and instructed my parents to pick up Ping at the county jail. He was freed on bail. Mother went to the bathroom and loudly vomited. Father was praying to the Buddha statue in our living room. They were dressed in their best clothes as if they were going to a wedding banquet. Maybe life would get back to normal? I sat by the window. I wondered if I could ever heal the wound within me. In my mind's eye I shrank the Judge's black robe into a tiny ball. Then I hid myself in my dark room, drinking until I passed out. Thoughts ran back and forth, unthinkable thoughts. I knew Ping and I were both caught in a web of rage.

Thirty years later, I visited Ping in Shanghai. He told me about that fatal night. He revealed the secret, which he kept in his heart for years. He said he witnessed someone cut the villain thirty nine times with a Japanese Samurai knife …

"Chen Chin Shui was the dirtiest bastard you ever met in your life," Ping was drunk on four sixteen-ounce bottles of beer. He slurred his words and his eyes were bloodshot. I didn't feel sorry for him.

"He was twenty nine years old at that time, that bastard, that son of a turtle, egg of a mixed breed. If he had grudges against the Mandarins, he should fight like a man. But he took advantage of the little Mandarin boys. Those ten or eleven year old boys were still innocent and tender. Chen had them kidnapped and raped in the rice field while they were crying to the deaf Heaven and mute Earth. We met in front of the movie theater on Main Street. The red neon sign of the "Star Theater" shone brightly in the middle of the sky, attracting people like moths to light. Under the sign were food stalls, fruit drink stands, game houses, and pet stores with birds in cages, sugarcane juice bars and people crowded in large groups.

"The moon was full. You could smell the air mixed with sweat. Loud pop music played through the broken speakers of the theater, mixing in with the traffic car horns. It was a camouflage of busy lives. Neon lights flashed green, yellow, blue, and red. Red was what I saw."

Who was responsible? We were the result of corrupt social conditions, leftovers from the perversions of wars, which kept China in turmoil. Would tears ever wash out the poisonous wound?

Television created a new environment although I remained in the iron-grip of my family I breathed differently when I went to work.

In Kung Fu movies I had to do a lot of flying. Production would hook me up to a harness, rig me onto a tree and fly me through the woods holding a sword pointed upwards. Of course, there were many takes before the director was satisfied. One time while I was flying a tree branch knocked my sword out of my hand, I began to smile, which was not what the script called for. It was hard to be serious. I was told to jump from the rooftop of an old temple set into a safety net pretending I was flying down. I would crack up laughing causing the director to throw a tantrum. Most of the time, I acted the choreography of the stage fight. Today the rigs for flying are sophisticated enabling actors to actually believe they have the power to fly.

From age thirteen to twenty I was expected to choreograph a dance a week for television. I was paid to dance my own creations. When ideas ran dry Mother would sit up with me until something cooked. I knew our circumstances did not allow me to quit.

When Father lost his job he formed the Yung Yung Tsuai Dance Company and School. Soon I was too much under everyone's thumb. I thought I could shift my lifestyle find something 'real', move away from the star who was in reality an empty shell. So I attended The Home Economic College and studied fashion design. Two years later I withdrew from the college and returned to dance and film. My attempts to move away from dance were really feeble efforts to escape my family.

By then I was no longer interested in Chinese culture. Everything Western and American held a fascination for me. Taiwan had modernized. Western pop culture, blue jeans and Hollywood movies were everywhere. I fell in love with two American dancers: Ruth St. Denise and Isadora Duncan.

I would attempt to imitate Ruth St. Denise, who was influenced by Egyptian art and Asian cultures. The image of her Oriental goddess was so powerful. It took my breath away. I made up dances about Buddhist monks and Zen gardens. My Asian culture flipped on its own image. Never once did I pause to check the motivation and source of my imagination. I never thought I could be exotic to a westerner's mind. Years later in America, I worked as an "exotic" Chinese dancer to make some money. Being Chinese was an abstract concept, "I am a human being." I could not see the slanted eyes, flat nose and broken English accent. In my mind I could eat a beefsteak the same as any Westerner, even though a steak was entirely exotic while I was growing up in Taiwan. The cultures were to cross throughout my lifetime.

When Ruth St. Denise married Ted Shawn, the father of modern dance, a new school was born. Subsequently, Doris Humphrey and Martha Graham took up the torch to glorify the art of modern dance. Both women established their own unique techniques.

Isadora grew up in America at the turn of the 20th century. She turned away from her Americana traditions when she traveled to Europe in search of her ancestral roots. She became infatuated with the Greek Myths and danced bare-foot in Greek tunic costumes. She moved freely and gracefully with her long limbs and abandoned expressions. Her movements were simple and basic, but combining the basic skips and turns she transformed herself. She too was a God-dess. At home, I began to drape white sheets around me. I danced around the living room ala Isadora. I took to smoking cigarettes in dark alleys, like characters in film noir. I painted my bedroom psychedelic colors. This drove Mother crazy. She could not understand. This was the beginning of her reading my diary behind my back.

During the Sixties Western society won the upper hand. I started to learn tap dancing and Jazz. Stravinsky, Debussy, Hayden, and Bach were the household names among my school friends. Presley, Dylan and the Beetles sold their records to the teen-agers by the thousands. Chinese opera became an antiquated subject, performed once a year for an elite group. The population welcomed the Hollywood invasion along with McDonald's and Coca Cola.

I went to the American Army base to learn to tap. I gave myself the name of Marguerite. Sometimes I would refer to "Marguerite" in my diary: "Marguerite is thinking of taking her life."

No pals, no lovers for me. I was not permitted to interact with Taiwanese men. Older men reminded me of my father. Young men in uniforms sickened me. There were no male dancers in my society. And then I had a tremendous inferiority feeling left over from childhood. If they got to know me they would reject me anyhow. I was a property. And as a property I had seemingly failed the perfection test according to Mother's ongoing comments as to my diminutive, doll-like size, which to her mind was a serious minus. There were moments I feared they would take me in my sleep to stretch and pull my limbs. Would a fox protect me then?

The feeling of being trapped accelerated. If I dreamt of leaving it was not escaping to another country. It was running away, high up into the mountains. I would be a nomad and take my chances for survival. Nothing was of this world. 'Grandma was right: I was a little dead-slave girl.'

◆   ◆   ◆

There were nights I would write in my diary, fall asleep, and then, awaken to sleep-walk. I would see myself float up out of bed without any control of where I was going or what I was doing. A spectral figure walking aimlessly. The ground was not solid. The walls I touched were unreal I could walk through them. I would end up inside my parents' bedroom. I would hover over their bed watching them sleep. Their bodies turned to the side, curled up with their knees against their chests. Their mouths slightly opened. Their souls vacated. I stood tall and erect. A force I was unfamiliar with took over. A powerful shadow hung next to the two little children, my parents. My mouth opened. I wanted to warn them: "The show's going on, I'm not ready." "Where's my costume?" "Where's everyone?" "I'm late."

I tried to scream out. I tried to speak up. I was unsuccessful as if someone was pressing against my chest and throat. I really wanted to explain to them how Yung Yung disappeared when she worked. When I danced I did not think about myself. I was a mere puppet. I would return home estranged from the world. And so writing became my escape. Ugly words, ugly thoughts spread across my journal in angry ink. Black and red.

My parents escorted me back to bed.

◆   ◆   ◆

It helped my career to learn contemporary dances so there never was any complaint about my going to the American Center to practice. And, certainly, my rendezvous with Martha Graham had been heartily encouraged. I did not expect much when I went home that day with Martha's words ringing in my ears, 'traveling is a waste of time and energy.' After all leaving home was the stuff of fantasies. My skills secured the family's living. There would be no other world for me. Again I thought I had tasted magic twice once with Bill Carter and for a brief moment with Martha Graham. I could not imagine myself in New York. Telling my parents about the scholarship was more to show them my value. I continued to want to please them, to gain their respect. That night I went to bed without saying good night. But I could not fall asleep. I went to my parents' room. Mother and Father were sitting up on their bed arguing. I could tell Mother was winning the debate. She said she had saved two thousand American dollars. She would take one thousand dollars to buy me an airline ticket. I could have the rest of the money to start a new life in America.

All of my desires were buried. I had no future as a human being let alone a woman. If I could not be loved except as an illusion on a stage, and if my parents had no comprehension of my desires and needs to develop as a woman what was the point of living? My thoughts in my diary were of deep melancholy.

Mother was not equipped to handle the frustrations that battled in my secret heart. I had written down page after page of distorted feelings and twisted anger. She had discovered the truth.

Dear Diary,

You will not receive my answer
I came from nowhere, will return to no man's land
My body is the product of my parents' love
Marguerite's soul is the little star sprouted out of fire
The star's light might have been effective and even touching for humankind
Yet it will instantly be gone from this moment on

Once sunsets, so many twinkling stars blanket the earth
One shooting star could be only one sad poem
Then what?

Time is coming to a stand still
I would like to retreat to disappear

Why howl, wail or cry?
What silly fools?
So many twinkling stars
A little me? Who would care?
Sometimes I hold onto my skirt, weeping
I can't feel motivated to live such a life

I see darkness around me
I can find no way out
Rage turns my inside out
I don't know why I would love to walk into a vast ocean
But I'm confined in my little space
The thoughts of death haunt me
Why do I want to live?
All I see in this world

is a sad life without Hope?

"You must go," Mother said.

"How? Why?" I felt insulted.

"I see you are very unhappy. You must go and further your career."

And just as I had been afraid to fly out of my invisible cage, my world opened up when Mother, not a fox, sneaked in my room, and behind my back, read my private diary.

This time she overpowered Father. Yung Yung would go to America, study with Martha Graham. There was a goal. I was to return, after two years, to start my own dancing enterprise. In this way according to Mother we all would bene-fit. As far as she was concerned I was to leave as soon as possible. Her quick deci-sion was no doubt fueled by my diary entries. Mother spoke firmly, "Your father will find his own strength too, and make his business work. He will support his family. You go to America now. You're famous here but it's not bringing you happiness. Go get more confidence."

I was reminded Mother had been the one to push me out into the world. She said I looked so frightened as a child. I was physically ill and small when I was young. She worried about me. Fortunetellers had predicted I would not be able to live pass the age of ten. There were two choices to be made for me to gain strength. One was to send me to a Kung Fu class; the other was a classical Ballet school. Mother chose the Ballet because she was appalled by the thought of women fighters.

◆   ◆   ◆

For the first time in my life I was walking away from my family.

"Take care of Papa and Mama. Take care of our baby brother AnAn. Take care of yourself," I shouted to Ping, tears in my eyes. I kept walking toward the airplane. I was wearing a wig and a mini skirt. I carried a make-up case of Mother's jewelry. My high heels clicked dramatically upon the tarmac. Ping's face burning my brain. He had looked at me with such sad silence.

And so, just like that, the little dead-slave girl flew across the Pacific.

PART II
NEW YORK DREAMING

Good-by little yellow bird
I'd rather brave the cold
In a leafless tree
Than a prisoner be
In a cage of gold

'The Picture of Dorian Gray' by Oscar Wilde

Five

It was the last lap of my journey to New York. Father's childhood friend, Mr. Jin, and his wife met me at the Los Angeles International Airport. They invited me to a meal at a Howard Johnson's where they ordered a steak. "Is this all for me?" I was amazed by the portion, "Why it's enough to feed an entire family of six for three days." At the end of the meal I bowed goodbye, never thinking I would see them again. When I arrived in New York I was met by Miss Fu, a woman Father knew through Teacher Li. She was to be my sponsor. Miss Fu lived in a one-bedroom apartment on the upper West side of Manhattan. Her ambition was to form a Chinese Dance Troupe and I was slated to be her main dancer. Also, she had other fantasies. Miss Fu had me share her bed. I was oblivious to her sexual desires, so I frustrated her. Not understanding the circumstances I became edgy and reactive.

The cousins, Grandma's nephews, visited me a few times. They were already Americanized. How could I explain to my parents that Americans treat their relatives like friends? Besides, my great aunt was mentally ill. I was told by my cousins not to visit for fear of upsetting their mother. In truth my great aunt had hated my grandma.

Three months later Miss Fu arranged for me to live in a Catholic housing facility on West Twenty-Fourth Street in Chelsea. I shared a room with a Hindu woman who prayed nightly in front of her husband's photo. She would burst out laughing when I woke up in the middle of the night speaking to her in Chinese.

By September, I moved to an apartment on Fordham Road in the Bronx. There I shared with a Chinese student. She studied at Fordham University and majored in world history. She cried every night because her English skills were inadequate for the demands of the school. Soon I was alone in an unheated apartment during the holiday season.

I had no idea of Christmas. In Taiwan a military marching display would be the way to celebrate most holiday festivals. Here the Christmas bells rang in department stores evoking a dreamland full of foreign ghosts, more like an episode out of the Twilight Zone. The excitement from the city's bustling activities was catching. I looked out the window and shouted, "Shai Shuei La! Shai Shuei

La! It's snowing! It's snowing!" I felt privileged: my first snowfall. I quickly put on my boots and rushed out into the winter wonderland.

I walked excitedly up and down the hills of Fordham Road. My skin tingling at the sight of icy white cotton balls flying in the air. Patches of brownish green trees, bare to the bark, stood in the coldness, mixing the whiteness with grayish stone apartment buildings.

I had mixed feelings about leaving home, even to study with the famous Martha Graham. I was not thrilled to be let out of my cage. It was all I knew. The pure and stark Graham technique exhausted me. Martha was right. Unfortunately, I was unable to live near the Graham school on the fashionable upper Eastside.

From Mondays to Fridays I was taking one class at ten o'clock in the morning and one at six o'clock in the evening. After the morning class I would rush downtown to Tenth Street and Sixth Avenue to the Joffery Ballet School. There I would take a Ballet class at noontime. In between the ballet and evening Graham class I would hang out at either the Metropolitan Museum or Museum of Modern Art. I often sat in front of a Van Gogh portrait. I wondered how he kept on living and creating? I attended every event and special exhibit possible attempting to learn from the museum's collections.

I could not watch movies as I did in Taiwan. The language barrier made me anxious. People suggested I take English lessons as a second language. Others advised me to take speech lessons in a drama school. I registered for a few classes only to withdraw. I was unable to focus, the same way I fell asleep in my Chinese history courses in Taiwan.

I was never good enough in my native Chinese writing and speaking. Grandma used to blast out her Anhui Province accents, Mother talked carefully with her muted down Southern Yangtze River accents and Father blabbed in his mixed Mandarin with Shanghai dialect. Whenever I spoke up Mother hushed me for my unclear Mandarin.

If I got lost in the New York subways and asked for directions no one spoke like my English speaking audiotapes. The visual images rushing by me were unnerving. I was used to people of one color and similar size who wore uniforms. I was startled by the complexion of the City. There were Blacks, Whites, and Hispanics. People were tall, short, fat, thin, skinny. They wore business suits, dress skirts, Jeans, tee shirts, Indian Saris, African prints, and occasionally sequins and feathers. They had black hair, blond, brown, red and sometimes dyed purple. Eyes were black, brown, blue, green, and blood shot red. My eyes tired from looking. If I became drowsy on the subway I would wake up in a different borough. "Blue-ko-lin," I shouted at nobody in particular before dashing out of the train. Usually I found myself on a platform unable to board an uptown train. I would have to go out of the station, cross over to the other side of the street, re-enter and pay another fare.

Christmas and a snowfall would be something different to write home about. As I ran up and down the streets my mind was full of clichés from books and movies. I envisioned myself standing in the midst of a pure white-blanketed land-scape on a huge Hollywood movie screen, holding snowball in my hands. Eating it. Heavenly joy.

Dizzy with my little happiness I soon discovered life had other plans for me. I looked down at my boots in horror. They had shriveled. They were clinging to my calves as if they were going to dissolve the lower part of my body. The cheap, shiny black, plastic boots were from subtropical Taiwan.

I struggled back to the cold apartment. I began to bang the radiator with a pot in the hope of hearing a little steam. The banging stirred up an entire orchestra from the other tenants. Now my feet itched. I bounced about to keep warm. Finally, I sat down with a hot cup of tea. I leafed through my favorite book "Three Hundred Poems from the Tang Dynasty".

The sound of the telephone ringing broke the chilly silence. It was Mr. Chow. Father's student during the time we were in Macao. Now Mr. Chow was inviting me to join him for a Christmas party.

"New Jersey?" I asked, "Where's New Jersey?"

From the directions he gave New Jersey seemed very far away. I did not feel like traveling to another state for a party. What I needed was a place to keep warm. To unload my stress from the rigors of Martha Graham's dancing school. But it would be good to meet Mr. Chow.

He picked me up at the Paramus train station and we went directly to his American friend's big white house. They were not happy with my "party" clothes, so the hostess kindly loaned me one of her outfits. A flowery, sheer silk blouse and a pair of bell-bottom silk pants quickly replaced my tailor-made woolen suit with its long black pleated skirt. While I was waiting in the bedroom, I thought maybe I would get to know the person whose dress I was wearing. A pang of fear charged through me. I do not speak English. How can I make friends? Instead of my hostess Mr. Chow returned. This time he tried to touch my breasts. My heart began to pound for all the wrong reasons. I looked passed him imagining my hostess standing by the doorway. I longed to see her blond hair, her pale face. I kept her image fixed in my mind, as if she could jump out and protect me from being defiled. Fortunately, Mr. Chow withdrew his advances. I wondered if he knew I was a star in Taiwan? Not that I personally cared. I wanted to forget that Yung Yung. Perhaps if he knew he would be more respectful? Soon I was downstairs. There were mirrors mounted on the living room walls. Circular armchairs scattered about with colorful leather upholstery. A thick, large white rug in the center of the room. A fancy bar had been set up under the staircase. The host handed me a drink. I politely accepted. The smell of the alcohol made me giddy. He asked me to dance. I wondered why I had not been properly introduced to him. I did not know his name. Where was his wife? Where was Mr. Chow? Where was the party? What was going on? In Taipei when there was a party, the boys and girls stood against the wall on the opposite side of the room. We would listen to the music while checking each other out, although my parents never allowed me to participate. If there were to be any dancing, the men bowed and held the women formerly in stiff arms. My host began to squeeze me tighter, his breath suffocating. Finally, I pushed him away. Neither of us spoke. I ran upstairs listening to the glass shatter behind me. He had thrown his wine glass against the fireplace. When I opened the bedroom door I saw Mr. Chow and his friend's wife kissing one another on the bed. I went back downstairs. The room was empty. I sat motionless on an armchair longing for my bitter cold apartment. After an eternity, Mr. Chow appeared. Quickly, I returned to my itchy woolen clothing. We boarded the train back to Manhattan. Mr. Chow told me if I were willing to be his mistress he would see to my security. I would receive money each month. When I asked to be returned to my Bronx apartment he refused. I told him I was scared to ride the subway by myself at four in the morning on Christmas day. He thought for a moment and then announced we would take a hotel room.

Once inside the room Mr. Chow kept insisting I go to bed with him. I remained in an armchair with arms rigidly crossed, legs locked. Perhaps, Mr. Chow was not aware of my innocence? I was never allowed out of the house after ten at night. I would not have known what to do even if I liked Mr. Chow. He was Father's friend who I was supposed to trust. Well, he did not give me a chance to know him. Finally, he understood I was not going to join him in bed and he fell asleep. He was much younger than my father, probably in his late thir-ties'. He was fairly tall, with a round and rather handsome face, large intelligent eyes. I did not find Mr. Chow repulsive, yet his manner and attitude made me hate myself.

What was to become of me? I was an adult. The sweet smell of romance had yet to touch my body. My heart was cold as stone. What defrosting lessons were there for me to learn about intimacy? Why did I turn icy whenever a man came near? Was my destiny to be an old maid spinning bright yarn from a spin spool waiting for a fox to sing?

A translucent blue light filtered through the curtains. This was my signal to leave the sleeping stranger. Outside, the white snow had turned gray. An early morning sun shimmered through layers of clouds awakening the sleeping earth. It felt good to be walking. I asked my heart, how do I really feel about living in a foreign country? I missed my crazy family in Taiwan. Another wave of loneliness shot through me. Would I always feel this way? Like my childhood idol Dorothy in 'Wizard of Oz' was I doomed to think 'there's no place like home'?

As much as I was yearning for the familiarity of home I found myself over-come by animosity toward Father. But why should I be so angry? My parents had cultivated my dance career with full attention and energy. I enjoyed the discipline of dance. I was capable, maybe talented, but I did not know it. My body followed instructions. Living as a foreigner gave me a new perspective. What was emerging was a view of a robbed childhood, which I came to believe my parents had stolen. They had owned my gifts and manipulated my achievement. I was to become further accomplished in America only to return to their vision of what my life should be. Mother had been genuinely frightened by my diary. At the same time here was an opportunity for Yung Yung to become more accomplished. "Oh why didn't she let me die?"

◆   ◆   ◆

While I was living with Miss Fu, she had borrowed five hundred dollars from me for a business venture. She never returned the money. I paid nothing for my room and board, perhaps she felt entitled. My funds had run out and I was too shy to ask for the money back. Now I would have to search for jobs to support myself. I had ruled out Chinatown. If I were to become westernized in the pur-suit of transforming Yung Yung I must reject everything familiar.

In the early 70's there were very few people in New York's Chinatown who spoke Mandarin. Everyone spoke Cantonese. I was an oddity everywhere; Asian girls were rarely seen outside of Chinatown. Even the beloved Hollywood mov-ies, the Western pop culture, which had so captivated me in Taiwan, did not seem very welcoming here in America.

"I really need a job," I told Jean Lee a Taiwanese dance school friend who also studied with Martha Graham.

"What can you do?"

"I don't know ..."

"Did you go to college in Taiwan?"

"I went to Home Economic College for fashion design."

"Good. You can sew? I've a friend who owns a sewing factory downtown."

I was afraid to tell her I could not sew. I paid my classmates to do my sewing homework so I could sleep in the dormitory. I was busy at night performing for Taiwanese Television, working as a stuntwoman for Kung Fu movies, and choreographing for various nightclubs and entertainment groups. School suffered.

Jean Lee's friend's sweatshop was on the lower eastside. Every morning I took the freight elevator to the third floor. I sat in front of a bank of sewing machines where I sewed nonstop. My co-workers were Hispanic. I was the one Asian on the entire floor. I wanted to make friends but I could not reach out. We were paid a nickel a shirt and ten cents for pants. The clothes were flowery printed polyester designs with triangle-shaped cut sleeves and bell-bottom pants. To make a day's quota I needed to sew at least one to two hundred pieces. I buried myself under the pile of fabrics and sewed my life away while Latin music boomed over the buzz of sewing machines.

My eyeglasses would slip down to the tip of my nose while my hands shook. Sweat dripped from my forehead, blocking my vision. An invisible monster was pressing my back and pinching my shoulders. I tried to keep focused on the single line of thread. The lines jumped out and laughed at me. At every attempt to steady my hand the fabric began to dance. My neck ached from bending down for hours at a time. I began to see double. I was losing control over the fabric. The sewing machine was devouring me. Everyday Father's stories came alive. Father's ghosts were putting on a show while I was sewing,

At the end of the fifth day I began to collect the finished garments to turn them in for cash when I realized half of the clothes were sewn inside out. I panicked and I stuffed them under the sewing machine.

Thump! Kaput! The machine broke.

◆　　　◆　　　◆

I was taking ten Graham dance classes and five Ballet classes per week. The hardship was worth it I told myself. Where had I ever experienced anything like the Graham School?

There were three dance studios with wooden floors, wooden ballet bars, and wrap around mirror walls. Displayed in front of the first studio was the famous Martha photo shot by Barbara Morgan where she was leaning forward on one leg, the other leg stretched high behind her. A great round skirt circled her body producing the effect of being in midair in a spiral. One arm stretching forward, bending at an angle gave a feeling of melancholy. Beneath the stunning shot of Martha were double doors that opened onto the glass walled studio. A director's chair was placed in the center. On both sides of the chair were low benches designed by the sculptor Isamu Noguchi. Martha had used those benches to demonstrate her technique. On the right hand side of the director's chair another double door opened to a garden where an ancient tree cast flowing shadows. Vines peeped through fences in the garden. Martha joked 'those vines are dancers' blood oozing through the fence'. A large, naturally stained dark wooden Christian Cross, Noguchi's other stage set design for the El Penitente, leaned against the wall at the opposite side of the mirror. This studio was enormous. High vaulted ceilings. A grand piano in the corner. Thirty years of dancer sweat seeped through the floors, the walls. A tangy, vineyard odor permeated the air.

The two lesser studios were not as overpowering. One on the ground floor was on the left side of the hallway. It connected with the 'teacher's' lounge where Martha often rested. The other studio on the third floor was slightly longer.

The office where students rarely entered was above the third floor in the attic. The staff who worked there dealt strictly with company business.

The second floor housed another office and the women's dressing room where we took enormous pleasure showering after difficult and sweaty classes, and often falling asleep in the dressing room. In many ways I felt privileged. It was a precious time as it seemed clear to me Martha was ailing. She looked so frail.

Aiya! Buddhas in Heaven! Why am I working so hard to try to keep the scholarship at the Graham school? Do I hope to be a dancing star in America? I'll probably end up starving and homeless. Mother can fart with anger; Father can belch with indignation. Their high hopes were ropes around my neck. Meanwhile, I dressed for business.

I next found a job working on weekends in an Italian bakery on the edge of Chinatown. Due to dance classes my muscles were in constant spasms. At the bakery I needed to bend over frequently to stretch my back and legs to release the pain. I would squat on the floor instead of sitting. Sometimes I would lie down on the floor and perform a shoulder stand or head stand oblivious to my employers. I had no clue what went on in their heads. I did not know their names. One afternoon I was instructed to go to the basement to pick up some bread. The basement was a dank, dark space with cement walls and concrete floor. Electric cords and water pipes zigzagged across the room. Four or five bakers sat in a circle looking at some papers. The bread was stacked up on a shelf behind the men. They smiled at me and I smiled back. They flashed some pictures they were looking at. The pictures portrayed naked women in lewd positions. Fearful they would harm me I ran upstairs, grabbed my bag and ran out of the building. My next job was to be equally harrowing.

The Azuma gift shops had a policy of hiring students from Asia who worked without permits. They paid a dollar an hour, twelve hours a day on weekends. Lee Fang another childhood friend from Teacher Li's school who was studying classical Ballet brought me in. She worked at the Azuma shop until she was hospitalized. Her ankles had swelled up from standing on her feet. Lee was emaciated from dieting to keep up the image of a Ballet dancer's body. Sadly she had a nervous breakdown and was sent back to Taiwan. Would this happen to me?

The owners of Azuma were Japanese. However our manager was Chinese from Taiwan. The rest of the staff was made up of a Philippine woman and a young man from Thailand who spoke Fujianese dialect, a little Mandarin with a very strong accent. At first he brought me lunch and dinner. He helped me with heavy-duty work. Then he began holding my hand, brushing against my body when he passed by. Gradually, he became more aggressive, opening his pants and holding his crotch so I could see. One night he actually followed me back to the Bronx. "Take a dive in the deep blue sea," I pushed him off. At work the next day he said something about "pouring acid over some pretty girl's face". I told the manager I was quitting. She kindly gave me an extra ten dollars out of her own pocket.

I looked at the want ads. First, 'Dancers' with no luck. Then I tried to find jobs related to Chinese. I could find none. So I went back to the letter "B". There it was, Bookkeeping printed loud and clear. I can certainly keep books, I thought. Sit and guard books, make sure books do not disappear.

I announced to the receptionist, "I'm here for the job." She handed me a form to fill out. I thought this job is mine. "Take a seat?" She must have made a mistake. I was there to take a job, not a seat. I looked around I saw some armchairs in the room and wondered how was I going to 'take' a seat. I stood firmly, my eyes glued on the receptionist. She looked up and smiled. A woman approached me with a warm grin on her face. Her blond hair was cut above her shoulders and her clothes were tight around her slender body. For some reason her presence comforted me.

"Miss, am I pronouncing your name correctly?" She led me to a tiny room without books. Ah! If I can have a job, you can call me any name you want. The young woman gestured to sit down.

"Here are the papers," she glanced at her watch, "I'll be back in twenty minutes, hopefully you'll be done."

I looked at the papers, covered with numbers. Numbers? Math? A bookkeeping job was for someone who had to do math. I flunked math throughout high school and college. My excuse: I was a dancer who needed to skip school classes to study dance. I was in a cold sweat. I was trapped listening to my heartbeat. The lady returned. She took a quick look at the papers and smiled, "Thank you and goodbye."

Once again I went back to the want ads from "A" to "S". My eyes caught the words "social worker".

I am sociable, I thought, people like me. I am pleasant and agreeable. Some times, I can even show a little sense of humor. I am eager to please others. My English is not good, but it is better than my math. This time I could be lucky.

I went through the interview with ease. I simply nodded my head. The test of English questions was multiple choices. I did my old trick. I closed my eyes, recited a Chinese poem, which related to a Buddhist prayer, held my fingers together and received an answer in numbers in my head like Grandma when she did her Feng Shui. In this fashion I randomly circled the numbers.

It seemed to be a government job. I was given a briefcase and some files. I was told to go to a certain location. I needed to find some ex-convicts. Once I found them, I should ask them to answer a few questions written in the files and bring the papers back to the office. I nodded my head as if I understood.

I took the subway and got out at 134th street. Here was a foreign city inside a foreign city. I found the address. The building was dark. Once inside the dilapidated hallway I was aware of shadows moving about. A kind of snorting laughter coming from the corners. A man jumped out and tried to grab me. My work in Kung Fu movies helped. I threw my briefcase at the attacker and ran. I sped to the subway and caught the first train available. I was still running in my kitchen. That night I took a loaf of bread to bed. I cuddled the bread as if it were a baby. I ate nine slices before I fell asleep.

Meanwhile, I was moving from one housing situation to another. An adventure at first was now turning into a bad dream. Juggling the job search with the rigor of dance training challenged my newly won freedom. Without funds I was forced to move from the Bronx back to Catholic housing.

The next job was obtained through a classmate who meant well. She would never have had a clue as to the hell realm she opened up for me. This ordeal is best described in the letter I dictated and then left for my ex-employer:

"Lady! You were pulling my jewelry pouch out of my hands with an ugly twist on your face! Fine. You keep my jewelry but you got to let me go. Why were you in a panic when I quit the job? Why did you grab my jewelry pouch

as I walked out of your door? You hired me to be your maid but I didn't sell my soul to you. Your apartment was stuffed with ill feelings. I couldn't stay. I saw demons and evils drift in and out of your place. I was better off losing the jewelry my mother gave me, instead of my life. It's been one month I worked for you. I am glad it's over. I wouldn't stay another day! I gave you my notice two weeks ago but you ignored me. You insisted on using me, ordering me around. You wanted me to stay with you. You worked me from six am to ten pm with a two-hour break, so I could go and take a dance class. You paid me twenty dollars a week plus room and board but you asked me to serve you till my body dropped dead with exhaustion. You even asked me to hand you my passport so you could keep me there in your apartment working for you. You said I was a good worker and you asked me if I would consider being a professional housekeeper. Why would I want to do that? I am only twenty-two years old.

What do you want from me? You disgust me. You are a vampire. I came to America to be a dancer, and you drew me into your family affairs. You couldn't see me! You couldn't see anyone besides your own world. I had to witness your husband beat you up in your closet. When the police came and asked all kinds of questions I didn't know how to answer. They told me you were Jewish and your husband German. But what is that? What does it mean to me? What was happening in your family? What was going on inside of your rich American Park Avenue apartment? You were so mean to me because I didn't know how to respond to policeman's questions. They asked me if I saw anything unusual. Lucky for you I told them "no". I was used to seeing you and your husband shout and yell and hit each other. I was so used to my parents, my grandma shout and yell and hit each other. Then why was this time so unusual? You tried to keep my passport. I would have to be your slave. You could keep me working day and night loaning me out to your friends because you knew I was on a student visa and not allowed to work. Why wouldn't you let me go when I told you I quit? Now you have my mother's jade earrings and my grandma's pearls. You lied to the Graham school. You told the school I left your baby in his crib alone that I stole from your apartment. You are the thief."

◆   ◆   ◆

There were no agents or working outlets for an Asian performer. To work on Broadway required permanent resident status. It was not until the late 70's that

Jadin Wong became a manager for Asian performers. I was not able to work with her until 1980. Jadin was born in America. An 'ABC' (America-Born-Chinese). She began her career as a dancer and actress in the 1920's when she joined 'Forbidden City', a nightclub for 'Asians only' in San Francisco. She had married a Broadway producer. When he died his family set up a managing agency for her.

It seemed impossible to get an ordinary decent job. I had worked a few times as a 'Chinese exotic dancer'. I could not handle that scene. I decided to forsake the New York Times classified for the Village Voice. And there it was, in bold square letters 'Dancers Wanted'. The ad was for auditions.

Daniel Nagrin answered the phone. He was a choreographer and a dancer with an extensive performance background. His late wife Helen Tamari had been a pioneer in modern dance. His current wife, Lee Nagrin was a prominent postmodern painter, actress and a performing artist. Daniel had also appeared on Broadway many times. He set up an appointment with me. It was unusual to have a one on one audition. I did not understand everything. I relied on my ability to imitate, to do what I was told. He was impressed by my ability to copy him. I passed the first audition. Sixteen dancers auditioned everyday for two weeks. I made the final cut. Victory, I began to work with a professional company of six dancers.

Daniel invited me to stay in his loft for a while so I did not have to pay rent. He reached out on a personal level to help me. The studio was located on Broadway between Prince and Spring Street. Many artists had started to renovate the dilapidated, defunct sewing factories. They transformed the spacious lofts to dance studios, fine arts and commercial working lofts, and music recording industries. I was offered a basement studio on Bleecker Street for ten thousand dollars. I neither had the resource, nor the vision to take advantage of the offer.

Daniel was about forty years old. He had a grin so intense I could never tell if he was happy or upset. His jaw was square and determined. He wore a pair of thin-rimed glasses under his thick black hair. He appeared wise and mad at the same time. The work was exciting. Daniel brought in members of the Open Theater; he invited Jazz musicians and performance artists to collaborate with us. We pushed hard with Daniel helping us to dig deep, to express our emotions through movement. I understood too little of his language to communicate. It was difficult meeting his challenges. The memories from childhood trauma started to bubble up. I could not understand this freedom of choice Daniel was lecturing me about?

Six

Martha fell ill.

Her absence added to my general insecurity. Her presence, good or bad had been, if only briefly, a powerful influence.

During the day I continued to study at the school. Bertram Ross and Mary Hinkson, her directors took over while she was hospitalized. Diane Gray, Helen McGhee, Ethel Winter, Kazuko, Richard Gain, Richard Koch, Judith Hogan, Takako Asakawa, David Walker were among the teachers. They failed to understand what Martha saw in me. So the board decided to cancel my scholarship. I was devastated. That enthusiasm of working with Martha had covered up so much of my fear and anxiety. Now the master was not available and her colleagues were not responsive to me. There was infighting and some wished Martha would retire.

Besides Ross and Hinkson, Martha's younger sister Geordie worked in the school's administration department. Geordie liked me. When my scholarship was cancelled she told me, "Martha gave you a personal scholarship." Apparently, Martha had paid my tuition out of her salary. Geordie was loyal to Martha's wishes. When the students smoked in the dressing room between classes Geordie would worry the building might burn. I added Martha to my pantheon of worries. How could they do this to Martha who had worked so hard?

At night Daniel Nagrin became my mentor. In his view we were not mere dancers we were 'creative artists'. His methods were based on improvisation. Daniel gave us various games and exercises while we followed our subconscious impulse through physical movement. We worked five hours a day, four days a week, with an open house performance every Saturday. Dancers received forty dollars per week. Here, I met Jim Howard, one of the dancers. He was a student at Julliard, and he worked with Jose Limon. His real passion was acting and the multimedia performing arts. Our affair was brief but it was a turning point for me. As a twenty two year old virgin and a potential old maid I had been frightened of intimacy. Sexual desire and emotional yearning for independence were hidden behind my mask of the ignorant and naïve little girl my parents wanted me to play. Maybe, my fear of a sexual relationship was a disguise to stave off the guilt I was beginning to feel about letting go of my family's vision of me. Father might be more complex but Mother had no other relationship than her marriage. Women did not express yearnings for men. Women were supposed to be married off.

I had become comfortable enough at Daniel's studio to be willingly seduced. I had broken my virginity vow, which had been a loyalty ticket to my parents. How was I to explain I was taught to believe in old traditions? Girls should remain virgins until they were married off. Independent spirits were squashed by the burden of obedience. Expressing inner desires outwardly was considered a moral sin, a disgrace. Couples holding hands on the streets would be followed by laughing children and scornful bystanders. I had never seen my parents kiss, hug or embrace. Not even a peck on the cheek. They bowed to each other from morning to evening. And when night fell they faded into darkness. Confucius guided our lives. After my affair I could no longer imagine a life in Taiwan. I began to see myself more than the little girl image I had portrayed for my parents. I could no longer rely on them to guide me through life.

One summer day after a short recess we did a show and tell at Daniel's studio. Each dancer went on stage to relate their time off. When it was my turn, I first walked around the floor, and then started to run. Hitting the walls with my fear and anger, I began to shake. The anger ripped out of me like a tidal wave. Daniel asked me if I was lonely. I could not speak. In my heart I knew what I was facing. For the first time I saw the enormous challenges ahead. Career, marriage and family were on the back burner. I needed a true relationship with myself. So I chopped off my hair, wrote more angry letters home, roamed around the lower east side to walk off my restless inner turmoil.

I would walk along Mott Street, cross Canal Street to the north side, and enter Little Italy. My lonely strolls through these neighborhoods raised my spirits, cheered me up.

In the early nineteen-century, Jewish immigrants mobbed lower Manhattan. Very often I would pass an old building with Hebrew, as ancient as Sanskrit, engraved on the walls. I loved the Jewish bakeries, the bagel shops and cafeterias around Orchard and Allen. I went frequently to a favorite Jewish cafeteria where they served matzo ball soup, gifelte fish and stuffed cabbage. I was at home with immigrant history.

For the last two months Daniel's voice, Father's voice, Mother's voice and my own went round and round in my brain. I could not escape them. Daniel's voice became a broken record, "You know you've the right to do what you want. Don't just copy your teachers and listen to your parents." Father talked back in a rage,

"Who do you think you are? You ungrateful slave girl. I've made you a star. Now you dare to speak against me?" Mother responded with her songs, "Why don't you stand straighter and taller? You ugly little thing. Can you make yourself less sloppy? You droop down like somebody who is nobody." Daniel challenged, "You must liberate yourself. Do what you want." Father screamed, "Stop crying!" Mother laughed, "Put up a smile." Daniel's new voice. "You must change the way your brain thinks. You've the freedom to think on your own, not someone else's words. You must create the dances that are haunting you. Don't make a dance because you think it's a good idea or it's a pretty dance. You know I'm bisexual; maybe you're bisexual, too. Explore the possibilities." I thought what do you mean? I don't even know who I am. How could I know my sexuality? "Explore." Daniel argued back. "You must learn." Father said, "You know you can't stay in America too long. You must come home." "No! I won't go home! I'm changed now." "Foolish girl, you can't speak English. You can't even talk to the people around you. You're starving in that wretched country. Come home. With your reputation, we can make lots of money. Leave the land of the foreign ghosts." "No! I'm a foreign ghost." "I denounce you as our daughter." "I denounce you to be my parents. I don't need money." "You do." "Will you stay and dance for me? Or, do you want to dance for Martha Graham?" "I don't know. I don't know why I'm a dancer." You must learn to choose what you want. I don't know what I want. Go to my friend, Mr. Jin's house in Los Angeles. They will take care of you. Mr. Jin lives in Los Angeles, thousands of miles away from New York City where I live. Why do you speak to us like an American? You know you can choose your own life. You are our little girl. No, I've grown up. No, you need us and we need you. Why do you speak to us this way? Have you turned into a red guard? No! I only want my freedom. What do you want? I want to go home. I can't go home! I want … I can't …

Throughout my moving from room to room I carried my family's letters with me like the family jewels except nobody would be tempted to steal this precious cargo. I would read and re-read the letters looking for clues. How to find a way to communicate? Perhaps there was a seed as to how to resolve my inner and outer turmoil? It seemed the answers to my destiny were hidden somewhere in their sentences. It was like hoping to find food in an empty refrigerator. The more I analyzed, the more I realized they were equally lost but without knowing it, whereas I at least clung to my little self-awareness. There was always the hope they might turn a corner and understand me. I still had that need.

◆   ◆   ◆

Pearl Lang began to dance with Martha Graham when she was sixteen. A tall slim long dark haired girl from Chicago, Pearl was beautiful. She had large deep-set eyes, a soft round face with high cheekbones and a graceful posture. She was busy working to build another school in partnership with Alvin Ailey. Twice a year she taught the composition classes at the Graham School. Pearl would notice everything especially when a student slacked off from an assignment. She too, was a demanding and tough teacher like Martha. Her students benefited from her discipline. Our dancing paths would cross many times. The classes were huge. I would be lost in the back row my mind consumed with thoughts relating more to my recent quest for sanity than for the dance. I was questioning my life purpose, wondering if I should indeed quit dance altogether?

She asked me to work on a series of movement patterns meant to express deep emotions. I chose to work on Rage. For the first two hours I was unable to come up with anything real. The closest I got to Rage was Pearl yelling at me. My body would be hopping and leaping across the floor on its own, seemingly uncon-nected to any emotion. I was moving without the control of my muscles without any will to control the body. I was leaping as if my body had transformed itself into a robot capable of powerful physical acts. I was high up, flying in the air, ignoring gravity. But it was not rage. It was very much like the chaotic movement I exhibited at Daniel Nagrin's studio.

The next day I went up to the Metropolitan Museum of Art to sketch. But it was such a gorgeous summer day. I thought it would be nice to take a walk in Central Park. I noticed a long line of people waiting for free tickets to see Joe Papp's Shakespeare in the Park. I thought of Father patiently waiting for OO7 movie tickets. A wave of homesickness washed over me.

A group of Hippies were enjoying the day. Some of them played guitar, sang John Lennon's 'Imagine', others danced free style. They wore long robes, flowers and beads. They would be my family for the day. Here was a group of individuals who wished for a changed planet. I could be comfortable with that regardless of language barriers. I lay on the soft grass listening to the music. People smiled at me but did not approach. I was grateful to share their vision in silence. I saw them as a small yet powerful group who dared to express their yearning for peace. I did not know any one in America who fought in the war or was victimized by the war. I did not know any one who went to Vietnam or Cambodia. I did not know a Vietnamese or a Cambodian. The shadows of war had hung over Taiwan were too long. The Vietnam War was universally my war too. The gnarling sensation of fear mixed with agony from the previous wars gave me a taste of my parent's left over bitter fruit.

I imagined Father the same age as I wearing a tattered soldier's uniform, climbing a frightful mountain, fighting for his life during the horrible Japanese war. I saw Ping in his present military uniform, brutalized and threatened by the invisible war between China and Taiwan. I would stay in America. I envisioned butterflies breaking through their cocoons transforming to something beautiful and free. If I really wanted to change my heart I could not return to my family.

Heart must come after the mind. I must change my perception of the world to open up my mind. Why do I come to this earth? I asked. Watching the young people singing and dancing on the green in the middle of Central Park I began to feel joy in their idealism. It was my hope too.

Father was a decent man just not capable of envisioning a larger multicultural society. He worshipped rich, dominant people and despised the underdog. Everything was black and white. Mother loved us. Her children were the ones who should survive in this world. She, too, shared a black and white vision with Father. I needed to go beyond. I knew in the midst of my struggles I had to stay here where young people had a chance to fight for freedom and peace, where young people were not afraid to demonstrate to the government how they felt. It seemed the politicians had to listen to the people.

Seven

The letters I wrote home frightened my parents. I was expressing so much hate. They decided to write to our old friend Al Huang, currently living in the Midwest. They pleaded for him to save their little girl from the grip of the foreign devils. And sure enough one day Al came to New York from his home in Illinois, to persuade me to quit Daniel Nagrin's Workgroup, leave Martha Graham and accompany him back home to Illinois. "You'll heal your soul," he said.

I thought I had nothing to lose. I would still be in America.

Al was born in Mainland China. He moved to Taiwan in his teens. After high school his family sent him to America to study at Bennington College in Vermont. He had meant to study Architecture but he fell in love with dance. Martha Graham performed and taught at Bennington during the summertime American Dance Festival. Al had been influenced by these pioneers of modern dance. Although he became a professional dancer he had other interests. Al received a Fulbright fellowship to study Taoism. For this he returned to Taiwan with his wife Suzanne, where he became a Tao Master who traveled worldwide lecturing and leading workshops. He was associated with Allen Watts who had virtually introduced Eastern religion and philosophy to the West. He collaborated with musicians like Paul Horn and Paul Winter to bridge the gaps between East and West.

Al tried to awaken me. He thought I was wasting energy in the dance world. I could have a greater liberation. He spoke wisely about taking a positive viewpoint. I could not. After all he was Father's friend. It was not until I was to fully work out my struggle with Father that I would appreciate Al's wisdom. I lasted one month before I left Illinois on a short go around with the Jin's in sunny Los Angeles. Staying with Mr. Jin's family had not helped either. Again, Father's friends.

◆   ◆   ◆

I took a window seat in the last row of the Greyhound Bus. Watching the trees, telephone poles and electric wires speed backwards seemed to calm me down. For the past two weeks I had chewed not only my fingers, but also the bark of a tree. I could not stop shivering. The Jins symbolized the very things, which drove me mad. Mr. Jin wanted to send me back to Taiwan. I would not let him. He had enrolled me in a secretarial school to learn to type. He suggested an office job. I did not go to the classes instead I was compelled to run circles in a local park, periodically clutching trees. I needed to fly away. I needed to break through my own glass shell. I needed help, but not from my family or anyone associated with them. It had been a bad idea for me to visit the Jin's. They meant well but I could not trust them. I kept thinking do not let them send me to a hospital. Do not let them send me back to Taiwan. I wanted to make a better healing choice. I convinced Mrs. Jin to let me return to New York. I wanted to go back to the place where I spent a year trying to grow up. Why had I failed so miserably? I pushed my palms together interlocking my fingers holding my index fingers against my forehead.

Think about my family. How miserable they were. Think about Martha Graham. How sick she was. Think about dance classes. How exhausted I was. Think about the endless job search. Daniel Nagrin's words rang in my ears. "What do you want in life?" I could not answer him. I did not know. Think about people I met after I left Taiwan.

◆   ◆   ◆

I was on my way back to an unknown future wearing a plain T-shirt and black loose sweat pants. Patches of anti war slogans were sewn on my pants. My hair short and disheveled. My eyeglasses were broken at the joint so I had scotch taped the brim. I became distracted by a young man boarding the bus carrying a green duffel bag. He was wearing a freshly pressed marine uniform. His brown hair neatly cropped. There was a happy grin around the corner of his lips.

It was unusual to see a young man so clean cut, so well buttoned in his uniform. Most guys I met in New York wore their hair long, dressed in polyester printed shirts and bell-bottomed pants. Washington Square was jammed with people who carried little red Mao books. The men who slept in subway trains or stations were 'Nam vets, most of them drunk or doped.

The young man reminded me of the boys I knew back in Taiwan. I imagined Ping in an equally well-pressed soldier uniform, his hair groomed to the skull. Beneath the American boy's sincere smile was a trembling fear. Would he die on the battlefield?

The soldier came right next to me.

"Are you Korean?"

"No, Chinese."

"Do you speak Vietnamese?"

"No, Chinese."

"I'm going to Vietnam soon."

Silence.

"I'm going home to say good-bye to my family.

"How do you feel?"

"Nervous."

Silence.

Chin Lang Shin's face popped up. He was my high school classmate. After he failed the examination of a college submission he was drafted. He received his notice the very day we had our graduation party. He showed up at the party, his face a pale green.

"Where did you come from?"

"California."

"No, I mean ..."

"Taiwan."

"Sounds far away."

Again the memory of childhood military marching songs came to my mind, "Fan Gong! Fan Gong! Fan Gong Da Lu Chu ..." "Strike back! Strike back! Strike back to Mainland China ..." We sang the song of the Great Wall, "The Great Wall stretches for miles and miles. At the end of the wall is my homeland ..." Taiwan was under the threat of war with China for decades.

"I don't speak English ..."

"I can understand you."

"Have you ever been in a different country?"

"No."

"Vietnam would be different."

He tensed up.

"What is this for?" He pointed to the patch on my right knee of my pants. The patch had a symbol of peace embroidered with gold thread and the words saying, "Tomorrow is another day".

"It's for fun."

"You do things for fun?"

"Why not? How old are you?"

"Twenty."

"Do you have pencil and paper? I can teach you some Chinese words. In case you get lost in Vietnam, you will be able to read a few Chinese signs. O. K.?"

I wrote down a few Chinese words such as LEFT, RIGHT, STRAIGHT, STREET, WATCH OUT, and WARNING and so on.

Thank you, sweet little girl. Thank you for thinking of me ...

Don't mention it scared little boy. I'll always think of you ...

"Would you like to read a book?"

He looked at me funny like you read English but you don't speak English.

"What's the name of the book?"

"East of Eden. Here's the book for you."

I did read a lot. I read English with ease.

He took the book but stared straight ahead as if he wanted to find an eternity where things might be beautiful and safe. The bus moved on shaking and vibrating under our seats. He looked sleepy.

"Would you like to have more space? I can move to the front seat ..."

"No, no, no, don't leave me ..."

He stretched out next to me.

"Do you mind if I sleep on your lap? I'm nervous."

My lap was where comfort found his home. My lap said love could help to heal. He leaned his head down. He was going to Vietnam. Vietnam was not a country. Vietnam was a war. He was the same age as my brother and he was going ... I'm nervous, he said. I worry for him. I'm scared for him. Why, stranger, why do I care? I am nervous for the boy whose name I know not.

His chin sank down deeper. I wanted to wake him up. My throat closed. My voice did not come out. A tickling sensation flew through my body. He wanted to take my life to Vietnam with him. He was blowing warm air between my legs. I was sinking in a warm pool of water. I saw bright, orange-colored persimmons, shaped like women's breasts. I saw tender, white Lichee meat tear loose from their brilliant red skin. I saw myself in the schoolyard with dragonflies and lizards. I saw Chinese bamboo houses, mountains and water. The houses disappeared, the colors remained: lacquered black and red. I saw a stonewall stretch for miles and miles. Then my body was quivering with joy. He sat up. 'My turn'. I buried my head between his legs. He relaxed and closed his eyes. What was your name? I would never know.

When the bus arrived in Chicago the unknown soldier got up and walked away. Good-bye, Vietnam.

◆   ◆   ◆

The fluorescent lights of the New York Port Authority Bus Terminal washed away all vitality in the station. I could think of no one to call. Anyhow who would want to hear from me? I dropped my duffle bag on the ground and sat down. The air was mixed with smells of fast food, human odor and disinfectant, which was not doing its job. I leaned against a bright orange tiled wall. Soon I dozed off. There were others living there. Many with those little red Mao books who would periodically lecture me. I was never fearful on the floor of the Port Authority

The first night I tasted the feeling of being homeless. Sleeping amid the crowds pointed up my aloneness. And this aloneness gave me a perverse sense of power. I wandered about the terminal for three days. Finally the knot in my heart dissolved. I let my shame go. I called May, a childhood friend. She graciously invited me to stay at her place. I also let go of my fantasy about becoming an American girl. Soon I returned to the Graham School and resumed my studies.

One of Father's favorite stories was about a friend of a friend who paid a visit to America. When he returned home, he told everyone "don't go there." "America is smaller than Taiwan," he said, "There're only two blocks. It's filthy and crowded. People have no manners and no class. I spent the entire month on a street named Mott." He never went beyond the edge of New York Chinatown.

May introduced me to Chinatown. She was beautiful with a slender face and a pair of round eyes. Often she glowed in loving warmth. She was two years older than me. We had studied dance with Teacher Li. May had never participated in the folk dance competition or the heavy scheduled performance engagements. She had concentrated on classical Ballet. Her family came from Canton, China. Sadly May's father abandoned her mother and five sisters and remained in South Asia. May's oldest sister immigrated to San Francisco in the early Sixties where she married an American-Chinese restaurant owner. In this way May was able to receive her Green Card through her sister.

We danced in Chinatown. We performed for community events and wedding banquets. The Four Seas Players, a local community theater group organized by the Transfiguration Church was a favorite. The theater's director Sister Joanna Chan had joined Mary Knoll Sisters in Hong Kong at an early age before she came to America. We were able to teach in the local public schools, working as visiting artists. I fitted in.

At the same time I avoided set ups which could place me in the fame game. I purposely missed a performance for the Taiwanese Students Union. I knew many students would recognize me. I jeopardized many job opportunities to teach dance in Chinese communities for this reason. I was scared. I associated success with imprisonment. I had been loaded with emotional baggage for such a long time I had very little psychological space for my own career.

The Catholic Transfiguration Church hosted a Chinese speaking school. It was located on Mott Street between Hop Kee, a famous Cantonese Restaurant on one side and a vegetarian restaurant on the other side. Many Chinatown kids grew up associated with the church. Every Saturday, there was tremendous activity. It was here I reconnected with my childhood idol Lu Yu. He was one of the few boys dancing at Teacher Li's school. He was slated to be a movie star in a Hong Kong Studio. And now ten years later, May and I saw him in Chinatown. We were thrilled. We knew his talent. Lu explained Taiwan had been too restrictive. He preferred America. Over the years Lu had become a working actor, director and a drama teacher also with a unique way of blending Chinese and Western flavors.

At one point I stayed with Lu at his West Seventy-Fourth Street apartment. Two friends from Hong Kong already were installed. Each one with a boy friend. There were seven people cramped in a one-bedroom apartment. Generously, they offered the bedroom to me and piled themselves up in the living room. Here was the family I missed. They dressed me, fixed my hair, and brought me to their parties and to all the gay bars. They fed me, gave me advice, and supported me at a moment of profound chaos in my life. Lu never complained. He extended his helping hands with an uplifted spirit.

Sister Joanna asked me to make a dance for the kids from Chinatown. I decided to choreograph a dance based on the poems by Qu Yuan, a poet in Zhou Dynasty 500B.C. Qu Yuan was not only a poet but a high official and a politician. He wrote 'Nine Songs' to ask the gods why humans suffer so. He ended his life by jumping into the Yellow River because he no longer could stand the emperor's cruelty and corruption. After he committed suicide, people rowed out the dragon boats in an effort to rescue him. The people threw sweet rice balls, wrapped in lotus leaves, to prevent the fish from devouring his body. Every year at the beginning of summer, there was a dragon boat festival where people raced their boats and ate sweet rice in memory of Qu Yuan.

I instructed the kids to dance as the dragon boats. I asked Lu Yu to be Qu Yuan, May performed as one of the gods. Henry Yu and I were the high priest and priestess. Henry had performed with me on T.V. and stage in Taiwan. We were dance partners. Henry had joined the Martha Graham Company but only briefly.

The dance went well when we performed at Pace University. We were also engaged to perform at Alice Talley Hall, Lincoln Center where Henry did not show up. According to Henry, Sister Joanna received a large sum of grant money to produce the show, but she would not pay a dancers fee for the performance. We had to volunteer our time, energy and talents for the 'cause'. Henry could not see the 'cause'. I did not care. I was detached from the world. I was more like a robot walking.

After the Lincoln Center project, Sister Joanna cast me in a play she had written. I spoke Mandarin with a heavy Taiwanese accent, which she did not think worked. Sister Joanna created a mute role for me, which had its irony. It was perfect. I could be with Lu and other friends. On the day of the last performance I lay down under a bridge as instructed. I did not do well. Unfortunately, I fell asleep only to be awakened by the shouting from Lu and the roaring laughter from the audience.

Although Teacher Li had trained me in Chinese folk dances as a child, I questioned the authenticity of Chinese Traditional Dance. What is Chinese Traditional Dance? Teacher Li had been trained in Japan in classical Ballet. She invented most of the folk dances Chiang Kai-shek's government requested. Chairman Mao had knocked down China's traditions during the Culture Revolution. To affect a rebuilding of traditional dances we performed with themes for the well being of minorities using fans and umbrellas. There were the Mountainous Vietnamese Meao tribal wine cup dances, Mongolian chopstick dances and Tibetan clogging dance. I came to question the public's perception of these 'traditional' dances performed with fake smiles and dandy movements. They were really taken from early American Broadway shows and Hollywood MGM musicals. What would a traditional Chinese dance actually be? Our Chinese opera went back but three hundred years. Did Chinese women dance in public one hundred years ago? Women had their feet bound? (Maxine Hong Kingston suggested in Woman Warrior, maybe women's feet were bound because women were dangerous.) In the past, males portrayed the female roles in Chinese opera. Chinese folk dances sprang from the lower classes. Chinese government used minorities as a way to represent a populace China. But the point in fact was none of these so-called minorities wished to be Chinese.

I had been taught that China was a country with five major minorities: Han, Manchurian, Mongolian, Muslim and Tibetan. But weren't the Han people the core Chinese dating back to 206 B. C. along the Yellow River? Manchuria came from northeast of China and occupied China during the Qing dynasty (1644–1911). Qing was overthrown by the Han who established a Republic of China. Manchu Nation had become a dream for the last emperor until the Labor Camps, under the Communist party, reformed him. Mongolia from the north wanted independence. Muslims from northwest wanted their independence. The exiled Tibetan people asked to keep their culture and religious practice on their own land. The Chinese government would not grant this request. The government moved the Han people and the Muslims onto Tibetan land. 'Let them kill each other. We'll call it a rural place, unstable and infested with crime.' So the Chinese government arrested Tibetans who objected to the central ruling. In any discussion on this subject I would find myself in a no win situation especially with Chinese people, including my parents, my brother, my friends and associates. Reddened faces and bulging eyes, fists hitting loudly on the tabletops, fingers pointing at my forehead. "A traitor." Or the worst, "an unpopular radical". These words frightened my heart. Then I would close my eyes, shut my brain down and keep on dancing. Words were useless. Let me enjoy performing the quirky and exotic Chinese folk dances, the flashy Broadway show tunes and the modern dance.

Later, when I seriously began to choreograph dance my skill came from modern dance training. But very often the themes would be related to issues of being Asian. After the Eighties when China opened its door many Chinese emigrated to America and the traditional dances began to generate interest.

The Graham School was in sharp contrast to this earlier training especially in spirit. Nevertheless, I was determined to make the creative leap regardless of the obstacles. Working in Chinatown with May and Lu became part of my life. My Chinese friends were precious to me.

When I received another Graham School scholarship I struggled to keep up the study of the technique. People asked did I truly dance in her Company? Did I not look too short and ordinary to be associated with such a star of dance? Perhaps, my parents were right to criticize me. Sometimes, I looked like someone who was run down by a truck. At other times, I looked like I was wearing pajamas on the street. The truth was I had never been a permanent member of the Martha Graham Dance Company. I was also not simply one of her many students. I did dance in her "Primitive Mysteries" at Lincoln Center the year she celebrated the Company's Sixtieth anniversary. Our relationship had been similar to the relationship between myself and life. Every so often it fell between the cracks of the world.

Daniel Nagrin had once asked me if Martha Graham reminded me of my grandmother. What do you mean? I thought. Grandma wasted her life on cigarettes, Mahjong tables and babbling in the kitchen. Martha Graham was an artist, a world-renowned treasure. I never consciously linked Martha and grandma together. But the evidence showed I tried my best to run away from both while taking them with me.

There were times in class I felt very close to Martha. She too had a broken heart. Why did I cling to the periphery of her world, yet somehow could not step closer for two decades? The gnarling sensation, which permeated the air, was too familiar. We had different life experiences but the clenched teeth were there, without mistake. A few times I dreamt of Martha. In my dreams she was surrounded by a pure white snowy landscape. I would have loved to believe I was close to her because I saw through her heart. But how could I? She was a genius in my eyes and I felt I had achieved nothing.

When Martha left hospital she taught advanced classes along with Mary Hinkson. A few students were invited. I was one of them. I trembled with excitement. However, after one month of intense study, my muscles felt so tight, every nerve ached. I went home crying in pain. I had intense cramps in my lower abdomen.

Dancers, like athletes frequently get injured. Their physical suffering was hard to stomach. I recognized Martha's genius but the environment struck me as overly severe at times even cruel. I was not willing to sacrifice my physical self to produce great beauty for a mere audience. Perhaps this was the reason people said she was mean. They confused her technique with the person.

One evening, Martha complimented my dancing. She referred to the cup of tea we had in Taiwan. After class, I went to her lounge to pay my respect. She told me she would like to see me dancing in her company. My heart leapt with joy. She said she would like to choreograph a new dance and asked me to stay an extra hour. I began to work with Martha for the next two weeks. Then one day I did poorly in Ms. Hinkson's class. Toward the end of the class when we were supposed to be leaping sideways across the floor, I fell on the floor. I had been contracting my abdomen muscles, crossing one leg behind the other, sitting lightly on one heel, springing up, balancing on one leg. Contracting in one leap. Then Boom. I was desperate. I saw the disappointed expression on Ms. Hinkson's face.

That night I began to bleed. I had had an abortion eight weeks before Martha returned to her school. I had an affair with someone I met at Al Huang's Tai Chi workshop. We were not ready to be parents. After the clinic abortion I wept uncontrollably. The nurse gave me five tissues and told me I must stop crying after the fifth tissue. I stopped crying as advised and went home. The nurse said I would start my period in six weeks. It had been two months without a trace until now. I sat on the bed worrying about dance class tomorrow with Martha. I was in severe pain. I felt my spirit leave my body. I could not stop crying and I could not stop bleeding. I cried for a week in my tiny room at the Catholic housing unit. Then the bleeding stopped. The crying stopped. I could not get out of my bed for another week. Curled up in a fetus position, I slept and slept. When I finally got up I knew there would be no more dance classes to attend. I called Shirley Wood, a Gestalt therapist. She agreed to see me. Shirley thought I needed to dig deeper. She recommended Primal Therapy, which she thought, could unlock some of my childhood wounds.

Alec Rubin's Primal Therapy and Theater Encounter workshop was a third floor walk-up on the upper Westside. A tall fellow, with shoulder length, dark curly hair stood in the doorway. He smiled at me. His eyes shining, his teeth flashing. He had a glow like sunshine. I was instantly inspired. He wore a pair of dark blue sweat pants. I passed him quickly. It was a small, dimly lit studio. About twenty people lay on mats scattered about the floor. They were screaming, yelling and crying. It might have been a disturbing scene to someone else, I felt at home. Someone told me it had been Billie Holiday's studio. Well, the studio was still singing the blues. People were calling for their mommy and daddy. I got down on one of the mats, my legs tightly crossed, hands clenched. Alec Rubin was a middle-aged man who attracted young people to him. Alec came over to me. He knelt down whispering for me to unlock my legs, unclench my hands, to relax. He led us through many exercises to get in touch with the famous 'inner child'. One of the exercises required a partner. Before I reacted or allowed this to upset me, the fellow who had smiled at me popped over. He introduced himself, Martin Lerner. He was twenty-one and he was Jewish. I told him I was Yung Yung, twenty-four and Chinese. His eyes sparkled. He said he did not know any Chinese people. I said I did not know any Jewish people. Martin distributed the mats around us. He told me he was building a house. The house was far away in the woods where no one could harm us. We hid under the mats pretending we were in a castle. He talked and talked. He was unaware that I knew little of what he was saying. But I understood him anyhow. I was content to be with him. He asked me what I wanted. I replied, "I want to go home." "But you are home," he said.

Our next exercise was for everyone to form a circle. Martin jumped to the center. He started to sing. He was an eagle flying towards the sky. He was a dolphin gliding over the waves. He gestured for us to follow him, to dance through the clouds, dive under the ocean. I was enchanted by his enthusiasm. For the next four hours Martin was a star twinkling in my eyes.

After the workshop, Martin asked for my phone number. I gave it to him on a piece of tissue paper. He called me the next day to invite me to a French restaurant. We drank red wine. At the end of the meal I went home with him. A week later I moved into his Greenwich Village 12th Street apartment with my possessions, two suitcases filled with Chinese dance costumes.

A few weeks later Alec gave us 'Shit and Fire', an exercise he created. We were to express our deepest feelings through improvised movement. Each one stood alone in front of the group. My turn came. At first I slowly stretched my limbs like a butterfly trying to leave the cocoon, and then I found movements for them. I gradually began to express myself outwardly, to tell the story of my embattled emotions. Of course I was a professional dancer but I had never connected my heart to these movements. I had never been proud of my gift. That was another Yung Yung who was considered a star, a young woman who had disconnected herself from her talents and was ashamed of the attention paid her. But now I thought maybe I could give them 'Shit and Fire'. I began to twirl and twirl. I twirled like a Dervish. If the group could really see my feelings I might be very embarrassed. I had spent the night making love with Martin. It was a passionate meeting of bodies and souls.

As I twirled faster and faster I wondered if I were inhabited by a ghost. A very sexy ghost. There had been no fear just pure joy. Now feeling power in my body I began to dance a dance of personal liberation. I was experiencing my movements in a new way. As I leapt and twirled I caught a glint coming out of Martin's wide-open green eye. It seemed to catch me like a ribbon out of the universe, gently circling around my body encouraging me on. My first glimpse of magic was due to Bill Carter and here I actually tasted it.

It was the beginning of my dancer's pride.

Eight

I felt no need to relate my Taiwanese big-fishdom-in-a-small-pond to Martin. He knew I had studied dance and had performed all my life. There had never been any value to my being a 'star' as long as I had experienced life as living in a cage. Whatever the perils in America I was free of that particular hardship. Whoever wished to be near me now would know me on my terms. Or so I believed.

Martin and some other young men were working for John Lennon and Yoko Ono. They helped the famous couple to move from their west village apartment to the Dakota, a huge old stone building resembling a European castle. The Dakota faced Central Park on the upper Westside, and it was here the anti war pop star was murdered.

Martin said when he met John he was lying in bed relaxing, reading the daily comics. The famous Beatle greeted him in his usual self-conscious apologetic manner. Anything Martin told me was interesting. I was in love. I sensed Martin's fascination with John and Yoko was their fame. I did not wish for our shoes to be filled with his star fixations. Whenever he commented how much I looked like Yoko I withdrew.

Other times I wanted to challenge Martin, "Do we really think we can know someone because a person has a famous name? Why must we make the performers more than they are? Do people escape their own reality, avoid facing their challenges by worshipping celebrities?" But I could not speak English at the time. Martin's fascination with 'stars' was short lived. The more I got to know him the more I could see his soul. As the years went by we became intertwined. Of course there were struggles, rocky, deep-rooted issues, but neither fame nor name was ever one of them.

Martin and I hung out in Washington Square Park. There was great activity around the cement pond, a mix of drunks, drug addicts, homeless people and NYU students. The statue of George Washington stood tall by the gate facing on to Fifth Avenue. Martin pointed out Bella Abzug's domain in one of the Fifth Avenue apartments close by. I was to meet Bella and her husband, frequent quests at Lerner family parties. After Bella's husband passed away she communicated with his spirit through a medium introduced to her by Shirley McClain.

We took daily walks around the quaint tree lined streets. The entire West Village reminded Martin of Europe, especially France. We would sing 'Martin and Yung Yung hand in hand looking for (the) God.' He would laugh at the way I put 'the' in front of God. Gradually I began to experience the richness of the American and European cultures. I realized China was not the only country holding five thousand years of cultural history. Furthermore not all Westerners lived solely for Hollywood movies, rock music and spaceships. Through Martin I was opened up to another abundant civilization, one where I could be free, where I did not have to store the perceived abuse in an already congested chest. I was no longer living in fear of a government, or a neighborhood. I had never experienced this kind of freedom before. Dictatorships, tyrannies do not allow you to do so. It was clear now if fear existed, it was fear of myself—my inner demons.

One day Martin's father, Irving, dropped in to see Martin. I was sitting on the bed and he mentioned to Martin, "That girl looks lost." I imagine the effect of Primal Therapy had left my face drained of color, my eyes dull. I began to think my misery was a bit comic.

Martin was interested in all things Eastern, especially Tai Chi and Zen Meditation. When Al Huang invited me to be his assistant at a summer workshop he was leading at Bingham Young University in Utah I was honored he had thought of me. Martin was eager to participate in the Tai Chi classes. He arranged to deliver a car, thereby not having to pay for transportation out there. Martin liked to drive and I was the perfect passenger. It was a great way to see the country. We were very near our destination when we decided to smoke a joint. Martin pulled over. We relaxed and soon we were making love. "Oops." A young patrolman poked his head in the car. His face turned red as a pork liver and he sped away. Twenty minutes later we were back on the road, this time speeding. A state trooper chased us down. I was stoned thinking the young policeman was coming back to kill us. Instead an older state trooper ordered us to follow him back to the police station. We were informed if we did not pay the fines we would have to stay in jail for the night. Martin gave them our last fifty dollars. Now we were dependent on the car's deposit to be returned by the owner of the vehicle or we would be without funds.

We arrived at our destination to find a sign instructing us they were on vacation. There it was we were unable to get our deposit back. Martin and I sat by a little stream wondering if we had been taken when a middle-aged couple stopped their car to enquire if we needed help. They were, of course, Mormons who generously took us home and settled us in their guestroom for the weekend.

That night I was in a panic. Father's ghost's stories replayed in my head. "Twilight Zone" was our family's favorite show in Taiwan. Now I was in a stranger zone with real empty highways, patrol cars, a mid-Western American jail and a white haired, blue eyed couple with a basement full of canned food and Jesus Christ symbols. What if they were ghosts or monsters going to eat us alive? At midnight when the church bell rang I pulled a chair to the window in case I needed to jump out.

"What are you doing?" Martin asked. I looked up and saw the long curly haired boy sitting crossed legs in his Zen meditation position.

"Jumping out of the window in case they are monsters."

We burst out laughing. Martin would continue to struggle to get his father's approval and I would continue to jump out of the web of Father's ghosts.

When we returned to Manhattan Martin wanted me to see 'Equus' on Broadway. The play starred Anthony Perkins as the psychiatrist, Martin Dysart. I was impressed, the stage set, the lighting design, the orchestra, the well dressed audience, the chandelier above and the red carpet below. I was excited by the actor who portrayed the young patient, Alan Strang. It was a story about man's need to worship and the distortions society forces on that need. The story unfolded through the boy's therapy sessions.

Why did the boy violently blind six horses? The young man turned to a stage horse while he talked to his psychiatrist. He began to gallop around the stage; head high, chest lifted, legs prancing, feet pointed as horse's hoofs. I sat there enthralled not understanding most of the dialogue or the true meaning of the play. What I thought I understood was the boy's heart from the way he moved on stage. I too had been bound and confused by that expectation.

While the horse pranced and pranced I envisioned a change in the stage set. I saw a different lighting design that had created three rings. I saw my family house set upstage on the right by the third ring, in a pool of dim light. Father was in a soldier uniform, rifle, boots, hat. He was marching, pacing, defending Grandma who was a queen on a throne on top of the roof singing a fox song. Mother danced Hollywood musical steps. She was busy decorating the barb-wired fence with pink smiling dolls, dressed as her children. Father, Mother and Grandma were tightly bundled together by a red ribbon in the corner yet their dark shadows stretched upwards looming large on the sky blue curtain behind them.

Beyond the barb-wired fence Martha Graham sat on a pedestal in the center of a second ring, her black and red Clytemnestra costume draped gracefully around her slim figure. A tall blindfolded male dancer hopped across the stage on a tall staff. A dozen horses danced around her in a fury. Martha Graham led her stallions in a circle of promenade. They tripped the light so fantastic they took away the audience's breathe. But a giant powerful Martha Graham reined her horses in the grip of her crippled arthritic hands.

I was prancing wild in the first ring where there was no boundary. Gradually, wings grew from me as I started to soar over the land of freedom, the land of Oz. Flying over the Niagara Falls, gliding through the trails on Appalachia, floating up the Mississippi River, high above the Grand Canyon, the Golden Bridge in San Francisco, and finally the Hollywood of my childhood dreamland. As I flew back towards the statue of Liberty my eyes went blind. I identified with the boy's tormented primal need to worship. I saw the tormenting forces within me. I wanted to please my parents, Grandma and Martha Graham. I had put them on a pedestal before I saw their flaws. Now I was dancing away from tyranny, away from the repression of Chinese tradition facing the mirage of an American horizon.

Martin worshipped his parents, and what his parents represented. He too chased after the rainbow which his parents 'owned'. He too was confused in his battle to find his freedom to be himself. Is this man going to gallop along with me to search for a free spirit? Or would he blind the 'horses' to sacrifice his needs? I smiled. He squeezed my hand, "Do you understand the play?" he whispered. "No," I announced. Martin said, "Neither do I, but I liked the horse's dance."

We had supper in a Greek restaurant near the theater district. "This is the best spinach pie," Martin assured me. He repeated 'the best'. His eyes shining. I would not know. But I knew he wanted to give me the best. If I had had any ambivalence about being with Martin, it disappeared that night. Love came to me in the form of the best Greek spinach pie on Forty Ninth Street and Eighth Avenue after a Broadway show.

From the moment I met Martin, I knew our lives would be bound forever. At the same time I would try to disengage even though I knew I could not be with anyone else. While Martin was obsessed with his father, I yearned for 'home'; actually it was the nostalgia of captivity. I shared another connection with Martin. I, too, was haunted by my father. My burden was subterranean, a trauma which would take years to surface and in the process nearly destroy our marriage.

◆   ◆   ◆

Martin's family was having a party to celebrate Judy and Irving's return from Asia. They were eager to show their photo slides from China. I had met Irving now it was Judy's turn.

The Lerners lived in a secluded two hundred year old farmhouse in Harrison, New York. The structure was painted white. It was a spacious farmhouse equipped with a living room, a dining room, a kitchen, a sitting room, a maid's room downstairs and four bedrooms upstairs. A large swimming pool behind the house with a rolling meadow stretched out to the woods surrounding the land. A pond was hidden way off in the woods. Martin told me his brother, David and sister, Mary Beth played and ice-skated on the pond in winter. I wondered if they ever encountered a fox on the way?

When Martin and I arrived, his mother, a beautiful dark hair, tall woman wearing bright red lipstick, greeted us. She gave me a warm hug. She wore a long black dress, black high heels adding more height to her already tall figure. I heard loud noises coming through the living room, wine glasses clattered, people talking, Judy Collin's live, resonant voice caressed the air.

An animated crowd of over thirty people filled the house. They were tall, short, heavy, thin, their hair blond, black and silver. The house was furnished with antiques and art. A grand piano sat in the corner of the living room. Judy Lerner was the center of attention wherever she went. She shone with grace. Obviously, everyone loved her. Another imposing but heavyset woman seemed to hold an audience as well. It was congresswoman, Bella Abzug. Judy and she were best friends since their years at Hunter College.

I could not understand English well enough to know what was going on. Martin explained people were debating political issues. 'Nam was about to end. He pointed out a white haired man, Paul Sweezy who published a Communist magazine. His wife Zerol Sweezy was another beautiful statuesque woman standing out among the crowd. Paul and Zerol were super rich from Paul's family money. Martin indicated they could afford to be idealistic Communists. Martin then pointed to another man, "That's William Kunstler, the lawyer who defended the Chicago Seven." I nodded my head.

Martin's father handed me a drink. He smiled. He asked me if I was tired from the trip from New York City to Westchester. I did not know if he was joking or being serious. No doubt he was being polite. Soon, Judy called everyone to the dining room. It was impressive. A long mahogany wood table was covered by an embroidered white linen tablecloth. The antique chairs readied for the venerable guests. Candlelight, flower arrangements, butter dishes, silver utensils and colorful napkins enriched the table. The menu was equally rich, roast beef, potatoes, au gratin, adding string beans and endive salad. We were served espresso and tea in silver pots. There were four or five choices of dessert. I wondered why did rich people wish to be Communists? Would they really give up their properties, possessions and wealth to share with the poor? When this came up in later years, Judy would argue, "That's not the point."

I observed an East Indian man and his Korean wife arguing with Martin's parents. "They are Chung Ja and Cass. He's an Indian doctor from South Africa and she's a nurse from South Korea. They could not be married in South Africa, or they would go to jail, due to the Immorality Act in effect at that time. They are good friends recently married."

Martin filled me in. Apparently Cass did not agree Americans should turn Communist. I thought of my own father and his dangerous brush with Communism. How perfect Father would fit in with this crowd. If Father did not have any language barrier, he would be a more suitable candidate to sit at this table than I. Father was so efficient at debating. Judy would give him a run. She talked faster than anyone at the table. She held everyone's attention by her non-stop talking. Her opinions, her experiences, her expressions.

After dinner, we watched the slides. Judy gave a smooth upbeat description of the China trip. "The most amazing thing there's no prison in China." She opened her eyes dropped her jaw and made an amazing face. What about the labor camps, I thought. What about their Cultural Revolution? I did not dare to challenge Martin's mother. Being a Chinese from Taiwan was not very popular in Martin's house. Perversely, I was the capitalist and they were the communists. Mao was their idol. I envisioned a comic strip from which featured a horse face and an ox head that represented Communist Party members by Chiang Kaishek's government making fun of Mainland China. Judy had pinned a red banner of Mao on the wall in her sitting room. She was absolutely taken by the Chinese Communist' charm as well as the Northern Vietnamese where she had visited with Jane Fonda. "We used to get hate mail from the South," Martin told me. What if I were a southern girl? I was saddened by the fact that as humans we separate ourselves by such confused opinions and ideas. Why was Judy so in love with the Commies? Maybe she saw them as idealistic Utopians. The Lerners epitomized "Radical Chic."

I did not feel diminished in anyway. I was glad I went. I believed by coming to the dinner party I connected with Martin's parents. Judy was a beautiful, warm person with enthusiastic childlike energy. I felt cheered up in her American-Jewish presence even if our political views differed.

Martin had told me Judy was an atheist. She did not believe in supernatural powers. She believed in her own power to change the world. Good luck I thought no fox sang there.

Around midnight the guests drifted out, with long good byes and hugs and kisses. They drove off dreaming of a perfect world. Martin's parents retreated leaving us to lounge on the sofa. Martin spread out his long graceful limbs, "This is where I grew up," he said proudly.

◆   ◆   ◆

Martin had applied to Goddard College in Vermont to complete his degree in psychology. On acceptance he persuaded me to leave the Graham School and my other affiliations. He succeeded where Al Huang had failed. Well, I was in love. Martin was able to help me enroll as a student at Goddard. During the first winter in Vermont we were attracted to one another but we did not know one another. We were both still in Primal Therapy although I could tell Martin's interest was waning. Whenever I got down on the floor to cry, Martin would pick up a broom and start to sweep the floor. Other times when he curled up he would cry for his mommy, I would suck my thumb and rock myself to sleep. Sometimes I would try to have a dialogue with him.

"What are you going to do tonight?" My face focused on Martin's back. Oh! Come on! I've enough of this one sided conversation. Am I speaking to a stonewall? I quickly caught my own thoughts and sneezed as if the spirit would be cast out.

"Everything's fine," Martin's response was casual, muffled by his own-clouded vibrations.

Martin's greenish eyes could chew my heart out. His long curly hair danced in circles. I have to be careful not to be swept away by him. Otherwise, I'll be devoured by the Vampire. As Grandma said, all men are evil. I'll never let my defense down. I'm ready to pick a fight. I watched my thoughts float by.

Martin. You are so absorbed in your own world. But I cannot resist the temptation of caring for you. You know that, too. You play your cards with charm. You can turn the world upside down. I'll be just like my mother and Grandma and take care of you the way they took care of my father. I'll die taking care of you.

I needed to lie down. I pulled the futon mat out of the closet and plumped myself onto the mat.

"It's only Monday night," he grinned with a carefree smile. I was jealous of his easy style.

"Ta Papa Mama tzen yeo chian, Ta men ke yee lan lan de ba shi jie wan tze seo Shang," ("His mommy and daddy are rich, they hold the world in their palm and he can take it easy and play,") I heard my grandma's voice ring in my head. Grandma did not know Martin, but she would have judged anyone in that tone. I could not stop the replay of Grandma's imagined words. I tightened up. I wanted to scream.

"Monday is so hard! Monday gives me bumps. Monday takes my intestines to the dry cleaners. And Monday hates ME!" I groaned.

I was there crying again. The moment I cried, the world cried. I lay on the mat and screamed my guts out. I screamed about everything associated with Mondays in my bloody head. Some days Martin cleaned the entire house before I stopped crying. Martin swept vigorously. The house never seemed to be free of Vermont Mountain dust.

"Ta Mama tzai ta ho mein da je bien tze! Ta yeo chuo ta ba fang tze da seo gang jing! Ta Mama tzen hei jiao dao ta ..." ("His mommy whipped her whips! She demanded him to keep the house clean! She taught him well ...") those words in Chinese were stubbornly conditioned and confined within me; I could not shake them off. I did not know who I was, but my head was filled with evil thoughts. I saw myself turning into my mother criticizing Father forever and ever. I saw myself turning into Grandma, beating my brother Ping senselessly. Never let loose. Now I saw myself criticizing Martin and his mother with the same satisfaction.

Water splashed everywhere. Water pulled over dirt and turned earth shining clean. Martin stripped himself and jumped in the shower and cleansed his aura through and through. Then he yelled out, "Christ! It's only a Monday!" Even the river in front of our house heard him. After his outburst he paced back and forth, looking out to see if there was anyone coming to visit. We were living in the middle of nowhere in the deep mountain hills by a waterfall in Plainfield, Vermont.

"Christ doesn't understand Mondays. Mondays are too slow for Christ. Christ was born with a halo on his crown and Mondays can only sing the blues. You are Jewish. You don't even understand Christ!"

Tears dripped down my cheeks. I was kicking my feet desperately while I was lying on my back. I waved my arms up in the air, trying to grasp something from nothingness.

"No! You don't understand! Jesus was a Jewish Rabbi! You Chink!" Martin barked at me.

"Moishe, we're both from ancient cultures. Wake up."

"Okey Chink."

"Okey Kike!" The words were meaningless. But this little meanness in me wanted to explode. I was sitting on a bombshell.

"I want to go home! I want my mama! My mama knows how to take care of my Mondays. I want my mama! Monday night sucks. Tonight is a sick night. It's a slow Monday night. I HATE MONDAY NIGHT! Mama! Mama! Mama! Where are you? How come you were never there when I needed you? I need you! Mama! I want to go home!" My screams faded. The Cimmerian mountains behind our house turned dark velvet.

I could tell Martin was no longer afraid of my primal screams. In fact, he danced to the tune of my voice, in slow motion, stretching and bending deliberately.

"Monday sucks! Monday sucks! I hate Monday night!" Martin stalked around me, manipulating his body like a slick panther. I pumped my adrenaline with all my might. I clenched my fists, bending forward and back, stomping my feet like a Native American warrior. I became my grandmother, the witch. I sensed the power of my rage and I pushed the dark energy upwards, forwards and backwards. Trying to expel the debris from the past out of my system.

Martin swayed his head side to side, looking at me from the corner of his eyes, catching glimpses of me, in the dancing light. He saw a black cloud whirl upwards. I was ascending. I pushed my fury up in spirals. Fury turned into vigor, encircling me in purple light. Martin and I moved in a pattern of a five-pointed star, whipping the energy of light. Slowly we met at the center of the circle we had created. He extended his hands to me. In turn, I responded to his movement by curving my spine in a twist. Martin held me in his arms. We danced through the night.

I can be different than my parents. I can cast out the curse Grandma put on me! I can … I can … I can …

Those words sank down in my gut and settled for a slow Monday night that allowed me space for change.

"Do you still hate the slow Monday night?" Martin smiled like a wizard. I moaned, a beam of light sparked from the heart.

It was a cold fall day when Martin chose to present me with a silver ring and told me to be ready for a marriage ceremony. Martin wanted me to see Montreal and my student visa did not allow for travel abroad. That was what he told me. So we secretly married in Vermont and honeymooned in Montreal.

◆   ◆   ◆

It was early June. There was still snow on the ground. We had completed the spring semester early to leave for Taiwan on a student exchange program. Martin intended to study Chinese and Tai Chi Chuan. I was going to advance my studies in Tai Chi Chuan, Buddhism, Chinese painting & calligraphy. That was what we said we were going to do. Neither of us seemed willing to admit the Taiwan trip was mainly to please my family. Recently we had revealed we were married to our respective families. My parents were outraged we had eloped. They demanded I return to Taiwan with their unknown son-in-law. "We'll not permit our daughter to marry a Hippie in America. What if he wears a big beard and has his hair down to his waist? What is Jewish?" Father inquired. Some of Father's friends who had been to America informed him Jewish people really exist on this planet. Jewish families also have traditions. They won't turn their back on their children. "You must come to Taiwan for your wedding banquet," Father demanded.

Although Martin did not ask his parents permission to marry they had welcomed me to the family. Martin's father generously paid our trip to Taiwan for our wedding gift.

What would my parents see? Martin was six foot two, one hundred-thirty pounds of lanky thin muscle and curly dark hair right down to his shoulders. Their dream came true. His face was slim and narrow with huge hazel eyes set under perfectly arched eyebrows. When he smiled he flashed a full mouth of white teeth. Fortunately, before we boarded the plane the Chinese Counselor insisted Martin cut his hair.

I was a petite Asian girl wearing a pair of crooked, wire eyeglasses. When I stood straight, I barely made five feet. My hair was black and straight; yet hung wispy along the sides of my dimpled moon-shaped face. My olive eyes slanted apart above a very flat nose. My teeth were tiny little pearls set askew in my mouth. When I was a child, I smiled my entire face squinted together to make everyone else in the room smile with me. This had changed as I was constantly crying in Primal Therapy. My primal pains had engraved a 'lost forever' look on my face.

Right after Martin and I married, Martin had said, "Let's go to Asia. Let's go to Taiwan. Let's go to China. Let's go to India." Martin was eager to travel in Asia. Where was Taiwan? Were Asians all alike? Martin was curious. And, the truth was the moment I received my permanent residence status I was ready to visit my family. It had been a long four years. Martin had become my security blanket in a foreign society. Now I wanted to see my family, especially Ping. I wanted to see my little-fatty-hand brother, again.

The anger toward my family never overtook my ardent desire to see them free of Taiwan. For so many years I lived with the sense that their lives were in danger. We had witnessed entire families disappear overnight. The next morning-poof-your neighbors were gone. At the time it was merely the fabric of life. Once I was in America these episodes played before me like uncontrolled bad dreams. Now that my parents no longer controlled me I was free to help them. I perceived them not as ignorant but naïve. In the back of my mind was the idea if I could get them out of Taiwan perhaps, their hearts, and their minds, would change? And then I panicked as the plane hit the ground of Taipei airport. What have I done? I have brought home a foreign devil. Would Mother understand? Could Father accept? What will Grandma say? I also wondered if Father would terrify me? If Grandma would scare me? If Mother would make me feel like a dwarf? I did not want Martin to hold my hand. I did not want other Chinese to see Martin was my husband. Martin noticed the way I pulled my hand away. He laughed at my silliness. My breath contracted within me. I was invisible once more. We arrived in Taipei airport after seventeen hours in the air. We were exhausted. It was one hundred and two-degrees in the steaming Taiwan subtropical summer. Meanwhile, we were wearing heavy hiking boots, wool sweaters, Jeans and camping backpacks. We faced mobs of Chinese black heads shouting in disharmony. It was a war zone. Despite centuries of war, all Chinese tend to panic whenever faced with an immense crowd gathered in a small confined space. The anxiety fluttered in the air. My heart began to beat in irregular rhythms. Taipei was humid, hot and chaotic. I lowered my focus, separated my hand from Martin's grip. After all was I not with a foreign devil? But, the devil was my husband. More foolishness.

A few people recognized me and asked for my autograph. Martin was confused. I had never explained I had been a celebrity in Taiwan. He looked at me, "How come you never told me you're famous in Taiwan?" It had very little to do with me. Father's words rang in my ears, "We've made you a star. You're nothing." How was I to explain this to Martin? "Meaningless." I said, "Meaningless."

"Yung Yung! Yung Yung!" The entire Tsuai family was lined up waving at me. My father was yelling. He almost leapt across the wooden banister. Martin and I walked over to greet them. I nodded my head at Martin, indicating this was my husband. He returned their greeting by flashing his white teeth. What an exotic place. What an exotic people.

"This is Mr. Chang. He's my friend from the office," Father spoke to Martin in English. "Mr. Chang brought us here with his car. We'll take your luggage back," father looked for our luggage. "This is our bags," I said, pointing to our backpacks.

Mr. Chang was a young man dressed in a suit and tie. The change in young Taiwanese dress and behavior came as a shock. "He has a car," I thought. A few years ago everyone wore student uniforms, military uniforms or "chungseng" Chinese buttoned down blue jackets. Young people had bicycles or motor scooters. I had brought home a hippie life-style unfamiliar to Taiwan. At the same time, I was shocked by Taiwan's accelerated industrialization. By bringing home only backpacks I knew I wrote "primal therapy, marijuana, new age and LS D." on my face.

I remembered a specific night at Goddard College. Thirty people were tripping on wild mushrooms. We floated around the pond, candles flickering in our hands. Most of the young men wore Jesus-style long robes with tasseled strings tied around their waists. The young women had free flowing dresses. We were dancing, swirling and chanting on the school meadow, our long hair flying with flowers everywhere accentuating our free spirits. Young people sat by an Indian guru's feet to discuss the meaning of existence. Yoga classes, Tai-Chi Chuan workshops and health food stores that was my world. America had retreated from Vietnam. Taiwan was forced out of the United Nations. Nixon had visited China and clearly Taiwan had industrialized.

"It's O.K." Father said, "Go with Ping by taxi. Mama will take you shopping tomorrow," Father spoke Mandarin. Martin looked as if Father had said something very important. He wanted a translation. I told him, "just our clothes." I was thinking I did not come home to see my family turn so capitalist. The word shopping sounded exotic. I had not 'shopped' in four years.

Soon we were riding through Taipei City traffic with Ping smiling at us. Our bodies drenched in sweat. Ping described the day of Chiang Kai-shek's funeral. Thousands of people, dressed in white hemp clothes, knelt down on the pavements. They bowed when the coffin passed by. Their heads on the ground. They sobbed to heaven and earth to hear their wails. President Chiang! You brought us to this island and you promised you would bring us back home. What are we going to do now? What is going to become of us? President Chiang! We came when we were young. Now we are old and feeble. We have no skills for this adventure, this industrial society. What is going to becoming of us?

"How do you feel Ping?" I said.

Ping shook his head, "Imagine those people thought Chiang Kai-shek was their savior."

Nine

We sat on an old couch in an air-conditioned living room. I glanced around the semi-familiar setting. I felt relaxed and at ease. "I'm home." After four years of America, I'm home. I collapsed with a deep sigh. Was this where I belonged? I looked around. There was no air-conditioner before I left. Then, I saw a telephone sitting on a small table by the window. Once I had been scared of talking to people on the phone. I was frightened of voices coming out of tiny little holes without being able to see their faces. We used to knock on doors when we wanted to see friends. Much of the furniture was changed. I was glad to see our refrigerator standing tall and proud. I remembered how thrilled we were the day it was delivered. Mother decided it must be in the center of the living room on display. I remembered I used to get up in the middle of the night and walk to IT and stare. It was our first modern appliance.

Now AnAn was running around in the living room. He was nine years old, and a head taller. Grandma had left the household to live with a rich uncle in a luxurious house. Mother said it made her life easier.

"AnAn, do you remember your sister?" Father asked in a loud and shrill voice, "AnAn, come here and give papa a kiss," Father stretched his arms towards the boy. AnAn shuffled in a figure eight promenade, reaching the side of Father's armchair. He pushed his cheek to my father's mouth. Smack! A loud kiss.

"AnAn is brain damaged," Father explained. "Your mother is the one who suffers the most. She can't blink an eye. He's much better now. Last year, he could tear down the house. I have no idea where the boy got his strength. It must be drugs from those doctors."

"Pa! Must be those drugs! Must be those drugs!" AnAn repeated after father. Then he walked off in a circular glide, with his fingers moving like a Chinese fan dance closely in front of his face.

Mother elaborated, "I saw a fly crawling on the floor. I picked up my slipper to swat it. BANG! AnAn howled like an animal. He picked up the sofa and he smashed the sofa against the window. The glass shattered around us, I dared not move.

"The medications were wrong. They experimented on him. He was like a wild animal. It took six strong men to calm him down and tie him up in a rope. We brought him to the doctor while he was tied up. The doctor gave him a needle. My wild son was bounded like a wild boar to be butchered!" Mother said, a vacant stare in her eyes.

The doctor had said AnAn would improve with age. 'Something about hormones changing in his nervous system.' Mother told me he continued to be hyperactive. Twirling himself into a bush by the roadside, jumping out of windows to run across the yard, dashing through heavy traffic, hiding himself in various dark corners and crawl spaces.

Martin had no idea what was going on. Our positions were reversed. In New York I could not understand two thirds of his family's conversation. I would nod my head and smile like an idiot. Now it was Martin's turn to flash his teeth.

Sweet smells of burning coal, cooked oil, garlic, herbs and soy sauce wafted out from the kitchen shack behind the house. I thought of those deliciously cooked dinners, the warm lively gatherings of my childhood in contrast to their cold domination of my life. My family's propane gas and coal stove flashed signs of poverty. I was deeply ashamed. Martin once asked me if I came from a rich family, I told him yes, not exactly a lie. I was told we were richer than most of our neighbors.

"Come, have something to eat," Ping brought out a plate of fresh Lichee nuts and glass bottles of Coca-Cola. The fruit cooled us down to our bones with its crystal white meat. Ping had grown up. He had served in the army for three years. He was working for a trading company delivering merchandise. I thought he was much brighter than that, maybe a bit too stubborn. A dark cloud circled his head. I wished I could help him.

"We're going to your wedding banquet given by our neighbor, Mr. Lew," Father announced.

"No wedding banquet," I said.

"Why not? Mr. Lew is already preparing a ..."

"I don't want it."

"It's already set!"

I shut up.

"Why don't you let your father make the decision?" Mother came out of the kitchen.

"Does it matter?"

"Of course it matters. We want you to go with a smiling face."

I did not want a wedding banquet. I did not even know if I was really married to Martin. I wanted to lie down and cry. I was not ready for this. I wanted to hide myself and be alone. Was I really married to Martin? Why did I come home? Why must we have the banquet the night we arrive?

"Anyway, it's already set. We're going tonight," Mother ended the discussion. Martin looked at me for translation. I wanted to kill everyone.

That night we had the wedding banquet at Mr. Lew's home. There was turtle soup, fried squid, sautéed frog legs and steamed bitter melon. We toasted with rice wine. "Gang-Bai!" "Gang-Bai!" How we Chinese love to drink our wine bottoms up. Everyone was giddy and loud. Martin was astonished to see live shrimps crawling on the table and we picked them up to dip in wine sauce to be eaten alive. He ate and drank with abandon. Later he was violently ill throwing up all night. He was married to a girl who could not speak English, whose entire family acted like circus players. Deep down he wanted to go home and have a bagel and cream cheese.

The heat was unbearable for Martin. Whenever he lay down he soon woke up soaking wet. His clothes, the bed sheet, the pillows were drenched in his sweat. The humidity was worse than New York. Martin complained as though that was not a possibility. He thought he was going to die. My parents graciously gave up their bedroom, so we could have privacy. Nevertheless, Martin felt cramped under the mosquito netting made of loosely woven cotton and hemp that enclosed the bed. His claustrophobia accelerated.

Mother had given us a thin bamboo mat, which was rolled up by the bed. It was meant for us to lie flat on to absorb our sweat. Martin thought it was a blanket. One afternoon he had taken a nap covering himself with the bamboo. Mother called everyone to see. We roared with laughter rudely awakening him. Martin jumped up half asleep.

"You're supposed to sleep on top of the mat," I laughed.

"You're supposed to knock at the door'" Martin protested.

"Nobody knocks on the door in China," I said, unable to stop laughing.

Poor Martin. The humiliation was on going. He could not join a conversation. We had plenty of long stimulating outbursts of laughter. We talked loudly and fast in front of him insensitive to his feelings. Occasionally, we glanced over in his direction, "Wola ... Wola ..." He would look at me for an explanation. I would laugh and ignore him. I was home. Before Martin met me he knew very little about the Chinese. He knew take-out chicken chow mien and pork chop seuy. Now, he was in Taiwan observing people constantly bowing to one another, and smiling strange smiles. They yelled on the streets and pushed and shoved on buses or trains as if their lives were in danger. He wondered why my mother stayed in the kitchen all day simply to prepare family meals.

One day, we were sitting in the living room a child's frightening cries were heard from outside. We looked out the window and saw a neighbor beating his little girl. Martin wanted to contact the police. I explained, "No, physical punishment of children is an accepted practice here. The police will laugh at you and tell you it's good for the little girl."

"I can't believe we're going to sit here and do nothing," Martin yelled. I shrugged my shoulders. We did nothing.

Martin was facile with wooden chopsticks in a Chinese restaurant in New York City. But, he was confused by the manner we ate at home in Taiwan. We did not use plates. We held a bowl of rice by our chin, and slipped rice into our mouth with the chopsticks. If we wanted a piece of food we dug our chopsticks deep in a communal plate, picked the food up, and placed it in our bowls or directly to our mouths. We ate with our mouths full and slurped our soup loudly.

Mother gave Martin a pair of special ivory chopsticks and a fine porcelain bowl with rice. I had a pair of silver ones and Mother's were made of porcelain. Both Father and Ping used square shaped chopsticks made of white ox bones. AnAn used a spoon.

"If you want to embarrass your guests, try to give them a pair of ivory chopsticks and a plate of hard boiled quail eggs," Ping joked.

I encouraged my brother, "You can watch them chase after the slippery tiny eggs everywhere," Ping and I laughed. Martin self-consciously looked at his ivory chopsticks. Mother went to a lot of trouble to find the best to show hospitality. She did not understand what Ping and I were saying in English to tease Martin. My husband did not understand the significance of being given a pair of ivory chopsticks. It was the highest honor. Ping and I spoiled it by making a dumb joke. It was irresistible.

"Ivory chopsticks are the finest," Father explained. "They are the next best thing in the world," Father continued, "The best are the silver chopsticks. Silver chopsticks were used only by royal families. Silver could test the poison in food." I looked at Martin. He did not give a fart about Father's comments. He was miserable. If only he could see the humor in this ridiculous situation?

A few days after we arrived at Taipei, Lin Huai Ming, the director of the Cloud Gate Dance Company called me. Lin and I had danced together before I left Taiwan. He told me he was forming a dance company in Taipei. Would I give a few lessons to his company members? I gladly accepted the invitation. Instead of the Graham technique, which was what Lin expected me to teach I led the students in a Primal Therapy session and Theater Encounter games. I had the dancers lying on the floor going through some relaxation exercises, and then had them scream out their pain. Lin did not ask me back. It was disrespectful of me. I must have had an unconscious resistance to the harsh and demanding Graham technique.

Martin was totally dependent. At first he refused to travel about the city without me. He could not communicate and he was also disoriented by the visual images. The signs, hanging from the sides of the streets were hung in upside down fashion. The billboards were written in square shaped Chinese calligraphy which lost charm when Martin had to find his directions. The sidewalks were narrow, sometimes non-existent, so that cars, buses, motor scooters, bicycles and pedestrians were moving interlaced with each other, creating a chaotic mass movement in a peculiar choreography along the streets. Bus stops had miniature signs unreadable for Martin. One day he bravely attempted to be independent. Martin and I had spent the day in the library of the United States Information Center. When we left the center, I told Martin I would like to visit a friend. Martin said he wanted to try to go home on his own.

"Will you be Okay?"

"I'm a grown man," Martin flashed his teeth. I could tell he was dying to be alone for a few hours. We parted. I prayed for his safety.

I arrived back home around mealtime to learn Martin had not yet returned. We waited until nightfall. No Martin. We became worried. We went out in the alley. Where was Martin? My parents and Ping chain smoking, AnAn kept spinning around, causing Mother to yell at him to watch out for the heavy bicycles weaving by. Finally, we saw Martin ambling towards us. He said, "I was sitting on the bus surrounded by a crowd of Chinese, tiny framed bodies with yellowish skins. Their hair raven and eyes set on the faces like two small black dots, their souls shining through. A foreign odor made me imagine I was sitting among aliens. Time started to play little tricks where my vision slowed down and my breathing was thick. I looked around and people were staring. I didn't know where I was. I stood up. I announced loudly, 'who speaks English?' No one. I got off the bus and figured out my way back, by sheer luck."

I understood his disorientation and this time I was not laughing.

The night we were to visit Grandma Mother thought she should elaborate. "She chooses to live with Fourth uncle because he's rich and lives in a big and new apartment. AnAn has nothing to do with it. What a wretched woman," Mother still talked about her-mother-in law with her teeth clenched. Would I be fearful of this person who had called me 'slave girl'? Would I be diminished in her presence? This tyrant of my childhood.

The family sat in a circle in the living room. Mr. Hoo, our fourth granduncle was an engineer. He had graduated from Columbia University in New York City forty years ago. Currently, he owned a big firm and was super rich in ordinary Chinese eyes. He spoke some English and was showing off his skills by talking to Martin while the rest of us cracked the watermelon seeds with our teeth.

Grandma was teeny, about four feet six inches tall and seventy-pound. Her graying hair was tied back in a tight bun. Her sharp eyes sunk in her eye sockets and her strong jaw equally matched her high cheekbones. She sat erect with her proud spine supporting her small figure. "Royal Backbones," she would say.

Father kow-towed to her first, then one by one we bowed and showed our respect. She returned her greetings by lifting herself off the seat and leaning forward a few inches as a gesture of bowing back to us. We were asked to sit down on the wooden armchairs with their backs carved in traditional dragon and phoenix patterns. The sight of this hallucination, not the vain demanding imperialistic matriarch of my childhood prevented me from crying out, "Here's your little dead-slave girl now". I had never considered this was a different Grandma, the old-leaving-this-life grandma, despite my newfound compassion. That night I dreamt Grandma was plotting to kill me in a hospital. It was a stormy night. I was running. Grandma became a witch chasing me. I ran through a spiral maze finally escaping the demon. At home I saw faceless strangers in the house, mere shadows moving about. They warned Grandma was coming to kill me. Breathless I hid under a wooden table. I felt her presence. I was shivering thinking, "No! No more fear!" I came out from under. There was Grandma. I held her hands in mine. Her eyes shifted, full of fear. I gathered up the nerve to look her straight in the eyes. I hooked her spirit right there and then with my potential power. I said, "You've no need to be scared of me. You've no need to harm me. I love you." I woke up in an instant. Waves of energy surged through. I kissed Martin and said good night again although he was sound asleep.

A woman walked into the room, dressed in traditional Chinese peasant clothes. Everyone, including Grandma stood up. She nodded at everyone and gestured to sit down. She looked younger than Grandma and Great-uncle. Father explained to Martin she was Grandma's stepmother. She used to be a servant/slave girl but was taken in as a concubine by his grandfather.

Then a miracle happened. It came from my fragile Grandma. She laughed, "Your husband looks almost Chinese." And a good omen for our future together.

"We have Grandma's blessings," I said to Martin. I considered this a victory. I could never have conjured up what lay ahead of Martin and me. One thing was clear my position of importance in my parents' life had diminished. They knew they had lost control of me from my letters. Especially, after I had married Martin without asking permission. Meanwhile, Father was able to identify himself as a successful businessman. He felt better about himself. What made them change the most was their involvement with AnAn. To take care of a handicapped child had shifted their focus and changed their perception of the world. They had to swallow their pride, their prestige. They had learned to accept imperfection in life as a result of their love for their son. And it brought them joy.

Martin had dreamed of going on to India from Taiwan. I was game but we needed father to help us with the visas. Both my parents became stubborn on the subject of India. They were frightened. India was a country of poverty. How could our daughter want to go to India? How could this young, Western man who married our daughter want to go to India? 'We have to be careful. Remember how angry Yung Yung can get? Remember her sharp tongue in her angry letter? We will tell her there's no way to get a visa. 'There's no diplomatic relationship between Taiwan and India.' I knew my parents were lying.

For privacy we used the excuse of 'sightseeing'. Martin and I took short trips around the island. We enjoyed ourselves on these excursions, reverting to our basic strong attraction for one another. We went to Tai Tong, a small fishing village on the east coast. For three days we walked along the beach, visited the fishing boats, and ate by the food stands. At night we strolled the city where venders kept their booths open through the night. There were snake venders with snake soups, snake spleens, snake rice-noodle dishes. There were frogs and pheasants, shrimps to be eaten alive, turtle soup, eel, fish in all sizes, bowls and bowls of rice. There were sugar canes and sugar cane juice. There were mobs of people wearing shorts, tee shirts and wooden clogs.

One night we were holding hands taking a leisurely walk when a man jumped out of nowhere and started to scream at me. He cursed so loud my face turned red as the lobsters. Martin pulled me back fast. I was still shaking when we reached our hotel room.

"He was calling me a 'whore'. He said I was selling my body to a 'foreigner'."

Martin said people were having a hard time in general accepting interracial marriages. "We'll have to walk ahead of everyone. In South Africa they put people like us in jail. They called it The Immorality Act."

I squeezed Martin's hand.

"As far as I'm concerned we're two people in love," Martin said, "Think about butterflies."

"Okay, I love butterflies. I'm thinking about them."

"I mean think about the difference in butterflies. They've the same form but it's their colors and designs, which make the difference. People turn color and design into prejudice. They forget about the sameness of form."

"But," I said, "What about the Taiwanese? They hate the Mandarins, and we look alike."

"Oh that's political."

"Sure, so is prejudice." We were getting caught up.

"Prejudice," Martin insisted, "is the result of politics."

"Or," I said, "Maybe I just don't like you." We laughed and kissed. It was not going to be a real argument.

Shortly after one of our excursions, I began to feel abdominal pains. Each day the pain grew stronger. I went to see a doctor. I was told I had an ovarian tumor. Martin wanted to return to New York right away. As intrigued as he was by Asia he had no confidence in an Asian doctor's words. On the other hand my parents zealously worshipped the doctor's words. Martin compromised when he understood I was not about to fly to New York to find an alternative healing method. Father wanted me in a local hospital. Mother stood by Father. I was satisfied to be in the Taipei hospital.

In the back of my mind I wondered if this had not been the problem all along? The excessive bleeding, the pains I suffered when dancing. I was so exhausted I did not care. Father won. I had an operation and was hospitalized for two weeks in Taipei Hospital. Martin came to sit by my bed during the day and went home with Mother at night. He started to pick up some extra money by teaching English to businessmen and tutoring college students.

On our return from Taiwan Martin shocked me by choosing to announce his new plans while we were riding on the subway. He was returning to Goddard without me. I heard this news over the roar of the train. Ominous sounds coming from a deep chasm: "You're not going ..." he said.

"I'm not?"

"No," Martin put his index fingers together and then separated them in a violent jolt, "I want us to be apart." I did not know what to say. I thought we were inseparable? Wasn't I the one who fell ill? Was I being punished for this? I was shaken. I could not understand what happened between us. I took this as a meteor strike. I did not understand why and how he could do this to me? My husband was going back to college without me.

I had to find a way to go on.

I moved to the Primal Therapy Community House on Staten Island. I would throw myself deeper in therapy. Whenever I regressed some of my sicknesses from childhood would slowly reappear. Diarrhea, stomachaches, nausea, chest pain, coughs had been symptoms. Father's angry shouts, Mother's beatings with slippers and Grandma's verbal and physical abuses played daily tunes. Repression and depression had congested in my entire being. The so-called primal shouts and cries seemed necessary to relieve this stress. These sessions were held in sound proofed rooms. I never questioned the methodology.

I shared a three story wooden house with others. In the backyard was a beautiful garden, a curved brick path around beds of roses, peonies, hydrangeas. A tall oak tree offered protection. My tiny room faced a church. A futon bed on the floor, bookshelves lined the wall and a dresser.

Once Martin was back at Goddard, and I was in my new digs, he would call me and cry into the phone 'You abandoned me'. What? I would scream, "This is crazy" and hang up on him.

I was alone. Martin had left me for his college degree. I had asked him so many times, "why?" I never got a straight answer. One moment he told me it was his parents who pressured him to split, another moment he said he needed to be alone. Other times he claimed we were overly codependent. I was tired of caring.

Martin began to call me everyday to accuse me of abandoning him. This was strange: early childhood abandonment was the subject of his college thesis. He was angry. I did not know how to calm him down. He whined, cursed, complained. I could not figure out how his neurosis became my fault?

I needed to heal myself,

Every night I walked uphill on the cement pavement to my room. My legs heavy. I could feel my Achilles tendon stretching behind me. I had stopped my dance classes. The one dance activity left in my life was teaching at the public schools in Chinatown. Even then it was difficult. One morning I sat in the school auditorium facing over twenty-five screaming children. I was not a very good teacher; I simply did not have the energy. My body was dense and fragmented at the same time. Depression eats body cells, one at a time. To fight depression I must heal my cellular body one at a time. I began to fast. I felt light headed.

Karen and Leonard were good friends who also lived in the commune. They were not trained professionally but they understood me, they had experienced primal pains themselves. And we often shared therapy sessions. I thought if I returned to my parents they would force me to a mental hospital, as though electric shock treatment could cure me. Whenever I thought of Father I became enraged. For two hours daily I crouched on a mat in the soundproof basement howling 'I hate you' to Father's image. Sometimes I would switch to Mother or to Grandma. At times I would hit my body. Karen or Leonard discouraged this behavior suggesting I express my anger vocally. Memories were a blur. I would curl up; baby cries came out of my gut. Other times I was a little girl pushed against the corner of the wall with my arms covering my head defending myself from God knows what imagined beating hands.

Primal Scream Therapy was developed by well-educated, well-trained therapists. Conventional psychologists often thought of Primal Scream as a fad. But it worked, allowing many of us to vent buried wounds. Gestalt was a more here and now method. I had no sense of 'the moment' except when I was dancing. Primal was an underground excavation with loud explosions. Martin and I were founding members of the New Age generation. I struggled to understand myself; Martin looked for magic in the form of an older man, a guru who could answer his questions. This was a quest not easily fulfilled so he continued to search and as a result Martin found himself in several disciplines at the same time. He was scattered and I was scared.

I did not fully understand the English language. I was ill equipped to properly communicate. This was a major flaw which fed into my naiveté about psychotherapies. I trusted my colleague's suggestions. I was incapable of making an informed choice regarding what method would help me fight my way out of the rabbit hole of fears I seemed to be stuck in.

After the sessions I would sit in my tiny room sketching and painting.

"You never showed any talent in fine art when you were a little girl," my parents wrote. I did not think I was an artist. I was getting through the day. My parents knew Martin had left me. They worried about my life. I worried about getting through the moment. I regretted writing to them. They saw only the surface.

Martin persisted with his accusations of abandonment. He also began to lament about his inability to connect with the outer world, his loneliness. I began to sob about my terror of ghosts and monsters in the house, my desire to fly away. Then I would repeat the inevitable, "But why did you leave me?" He accused me of not understanding him. I did not hang up on these calls. In some way we diffused each other's pain and my heart opened up.

It was only a ten-minute walk from the bus stop to the community house but it felt like an eternity. I would stop to notice the rays of a setting sun. "You are my sunshine, my only sunshine ..." popped in my ears. Martin liked to hum this tune. One enemy at a time, one bullet at a time. His decision to leave was irrational but how many rational choices had I made in my life? I wanted to go home. But where was home? "You are my sunshine ..." I did not know what the day's primal session would be, what memory would push forward. Or what connection I would make between the here and now and my regressed self? Maybe it would be a break-through session? If not I would have to keep going, to dig deeper. I had nothing to lose. That day what pushed through was the reality of my need to see my husband. Was it possible he was in more trouble than me? I decided to visit Martin.

Martin met me at the bus stop with a fresh idea. We were to visit a small health food store near by. A couple dressed in East Indian cotton clothing lived behind the curtain in back of the store. The woman had long hair with a pink flower pinned over her ear; the man wore longhair and a beard. A toddler was crawling on the floor making happy sounds. They sold grains, whole flour, nuts and dried fruits. Vitamins were stocked along with freshly ground peanut butter, jam, tahini, soy sauce, apple cider vinegar etc. The fragrance of herbs permeated the room. Candles, incense, and Buddha statues. I breathed deeply.

"I'd like to own a health food store like this one," Martin said.

"I thought you were going to be a psychologist?"

"No. I want to live a simple life like this one, a health food store and a family. How is your diet doing?"

"My skin turns orange. Too much carrot juice."

Martin had not been the one to introduce me to my current diet which was meant to deter mucous, I could tell he thought he was losing his grip on me. I was confused by his behavior. Maybe, I was not attractive enough? Eventually I realized there was no particular reason. He was twenty-three years old. In his parents' eyes he was a child. What about me? I thought. His parents were not considering me. I understood Martin was under their spell. Why can't he be his own man?

I never confronted him.

Next, we visited a woman Martin considered a guru. She had worked with the Living Theater in New York City in the Sixties. At present she lived alone in a yurt, a Tibetan style tent. It was dark when we arrived. Candles were lit. A dark red Oriental rug covered the center space. Woven American-Indian wool blankets were draped about. There was a small, low wooden table, a single futon bed, and a few wool blankets folded by the bed. A water bucket and woodstove sat in the corner. The woman was in lotus position meditating when we walked in. An Indian shawl wrapped around her small body frame. She smiled at us. Apparently it was not Martin's first visit. She offered us chamomile tea and whole grain bread with butter. We sat with her in silence until midnight when she put out the candles.

Martin took my hand. We walked out in the dark where we reconciled by making love. And so by the light of the mellow Vermont moon our love was rekindled by the pungent smell of incense and candle wax.

At Martin's graduation from Goddard he suggested we move to Colorado. I convinced him to first come with me to attend a Primal Scream retreat in Saluka near Woodstock. Our old friend Alec Rubin was leading a group of thirty people in retreat sessions. Bill, a fellow retreatent told me he had some LSD and for some reason I decided to go tripping while primaling. I did not check with Martin for this trip. And it was a bad one. At one point I looked in terror at Bill's eyes. I was sure he was going to kill me. I ran to Alec saying 'Bill's going to kill me.' He checked my eyes. I heard people say 'she's so far out she's gone'. I searched for Martin but he was so furious he ignored me. "It's a bad trip," Alec said, "She'll come down."

The terror was too real, the extreme gnarling sensation in my body, too familiar. In the end Martin came to my rescue. He checked us into a motel where I was able to fall asleep. There was a lesson here for I had never glimpsed my inner terror so realistically. It seemed to be connected to a deep rooted fear of being killed by a man. Martin and I had occasionally dropped LSD. We smoked pot, a lesser hallucinogenic but none the less affecting the nervous system. We were getting high, which meant experiencing alternate states of mind which we had enjoyed. But this was different. I was not dropping acid under the direction of a professional. I was traveling solo between the cracks in the world without a guide. And although I had met terror there the drugs pushed me further inward where fear was home.

One day I would come to understand I must go directly into that darkness to fully open my heart if I were to be healed, or I would forever travel in that fear. That would be my turning point. But, that was in the future. Martin had told me that during one of his acid trips, his friend found God, and he found primal therapy. Maybe, I was going to find Death? That was how I felt.

Ten

In the search for self-knowledge, getting high, dropping acid could be considered learning tools. On the negative side loomed the possibility of addiction. Smoking weed had become an accepted social activity. Martin had been turned on in his parent's home by William Kunstler, the well-known liberal lawyer and a close friend of the family. The American Jazz clubs and the hip subculture who smoked in the late Fifties morphed into the Sixties' hallucinogenic society. Martin and I were experimenters who fortunately never got addicted, but the experience had taken a toll. Nervous system was too fragile to support the path of 'getting high'.

The Green in the center of town exuded the same energy as Washington Square Park except here the Hippies were aging. Young Punks trying to live up to the old Hippie tradition, but not quite making it. Tinker Street, the main drag had long been a tourist haven for weekend shoppers and day-trippers. A fantasy walk of unique boutiques with flavors from Asia, Europe, Indonesia, tie-dyed Americana now with a Tibetan influence.

There was nothing to doubt about the beauty of the Catskill Mountains and the view of the Hudson Valley which had long attracted artisans and painters. They came in the 19th Century to find inspiration. There is a saying 'once one lives on the land one will never be able to leave.' Many Indian burial grounds surrounded us. Their spirits capturing our minds. In this mindset Martin found Nature's Pantry, a health food store. It was smack in the center of the Village Green and it was for sale. He had visions of our padding around in Indian gauze—burning incense and healing the universe with health food. Martin who was still struggling with his parents somehow persuaded them to buy it for him. How was this going to play? He had no retail experience. As it turned out, his father constantly interfered, preventing Martin from making a decision on his own. The endless father/son conversations would begin in the sunshine, and end in the dark of night leaving Martin a diminished man.

We kept up our ongoing analysis of our respective parents. Private conversations became repetitive; I would analyze his mother and he would analyze my father. And then I got pregnant, at which point we became strict vegans, no sugar, eggs, and no drugs.

Although I spoke minimal English I read with ease, and I read voraciously. I retreated to books. When I made my decision to quit therapy to concentrate on my pregnancy Martin was over the moon. In three years I had not come any closer to understanding the ache in my psyche. I still attributed my anger to a 'stage father's strict demands.

Martin found a guru, an Indian teacher who taught Darshan Yoga. Dr. Kaushik came to Woodstock several times a year to give lectures and lead meditations. He was an Indian medical doctor who after a heart attack began to meditate. He explored the unknown by observing his mind in meditation. He emphasized the importance of reaching the state of 'silence'. He would call it, 'God's visit'. It was the first time I began to realize a quieting of thoughts and a flash of spiritual awareness which I attributed to meditation and Dr. Kaushik's teaching.

Brad, a close disciple of Dr. Kaushik was living in Woodstock year 'round. He acted as a surrogate guru so Martin now became Brad's disciple. He put Brad high up on a golden pedestal. The guru could do nothing wrong. Martin and I went to Brad's house every evening to meditate and sit at his feet and listen. Martin, young and naïve, tended to ask practical questions about what to do with the store, what to do with his parents, what to do with his life. A few months later Brad mentioned we never brought a bag of raisins to offer him. We started to bring box after box of food to him. Soon Brad sent several of his disciples to work in the store perhaps in response to Martin's nagging questions about what to do with the business.

Once Martin focused on the guru we had no intimate family life. Affection left our relationship. As our baby grew within me I was eager to have my mother visit. She could cook. She could tell me stories. We could have our giggles. Now that I was an American citizen I was eligible to apply for permanent residence for the Tsuai family. And they were willing. However the Taiwanese government denied AnAn a passport. They insisted he must be drafted at the proper age. We knew this could never happen due to his illness.

It was winter in Woodstock when Mother arrived. We were cozy behind our little store. Martin was comical. Often he blurted out, "Don't bother me. I'm pregnant." He began to feel nausea and dizzy in the mornings. Not until I started to tease him did he cease to act out my pregnancy. Once more we were high on life. Everything had gone well. Mother's presence enriched our world. With

Mother and Karen, the midwife, expected the night of our baby's birth, I felt secure.

On the fateful night Martin who had once said to me, 'Dance is life—teach me to live, teach me to dance' was able to fulfill his aspiration. We tangoed well into the night. Dum Da Dum Dum Da Dum! My belly stuck out one foot from my spine. I could not reach Martin's chest, but we danced. At one point, Martin performed with a broomstick. Another time, I waved the shawl from the back of the couch to dance a Flamingo mixed with Tango. Bam Da Bam Bam Da Bam! Mother sat on the couch rocking and swaying, watching us perform. Delighted by our enthusiastic energy, she laughed like a young girl. We went to bed at two am.

Around 4 am I had to pee badly. Water dripped out of me. I thought I had an accident. It was hard to tell if it was the fetus rubbing between my legs, or my bladder, or a bowel movement. When I looked down at the pool of water under my feet I realized the baby was coming.

I awakened Martin, "The baby is coming." Martin contacted the midwife. She instructed Martin to call her back when my contractions were five minutes apart. "Look," I said, "there's no time. Call her again to come now, the baby is coming."

By 7 am a blizzard had started and Karen had not arrived. A snowstorm outside and a typhoon inside. I vomited. The pain was unbearable. I dug my head in the pillows and screamed out. I tried to push hard. The baby was pushing, too. I could feel the little body trying to come to this world. Karen finally arrived. "Oh, my god, the baby is coming out." Without taking off her snow jacket, she helped me to push. One hour later, the baby's head came out. "The hair is black," Martin announced. Push hard, push, the hair is black, I can see the hair, push harder. But no. The baby's shoulder is stuck. Martin called the ambulance. By the time the ambulance arrived, Karen had helped me to push the baby out.

February 2nd, 1976, 8 a.m. Tysan (Black Coral) was born. "It's a girl," Martin smiled. Karen placed Tysan on my bosom. Massage her back, she said. I stroked her gently. I turned her over to face me. I saw her dark piercing gaze looking through my soul. It is my little girl. I wept.

8:30 a.m. I heard a huge noise coming from the kitchen. Martin had heated a pot of hot water to bath Tysan. It was good to bath the newborn infant in a warm bath. Theory remained a theory. Martin dropped the pot on the floor. Tysan never received her first warm bath. I started to feel dizzy. I complained about feeling faint. Karen checked my pulse and was alarmed. It was determined I was hemorrhaging. Martin called the ambulance again. This time they rushed in and strapped me to a stretcher. I saw Mother pale by the door. I was too weak to reassure her.

At Kingston hospital, they told me I had lost a pint of blood. They gave me a transfusion. I wanted my baby. They said no. The baby was not born in the hospital. She could not be admitted. Luckily, the next day the hospital dismissed me. Mother was holding Tysan when I got home. It was so comforting to see Mother with my baby girl. Tysan wrapped in a Chinese red, cotton flower printed quilt which mother had made. Both of them smiled at me warmly. Mother quickly handed Tysan to me. I nursed her. "Blood is the blood. The baby is now so calm and loving in her mother's arms. No one can take her mother's place," Mother said.

Years later, Tysan asked me what it was like to give birth. It's like taking a huge gigantic shit, I said. Any pain? I was questioned. What pain? I can only remember her warm little body cuddled in my arms and the sensation of the suckling. Of course one day she was to have the extraordinary experience of motherhood herself.

When Mother returned to Taiwan I began to help Martin in Nature's Pantry. It was clear Martin was not interested in retail business. It was really an attempt to fulfill his father's wish to carry on a family's tradition. Martin wanted to be an artist. He had once told me he had even wanted to be a dancer. He did not have any opportunity to study dance which, I thought, was more a dream than a motivation since he had two left feet by nature. It would be so much easier for me to carry out his dream. He would continuously talk to customers about my dancing ability. Through the grapevine, local dancers began to contact me. I wound up joining a four women improvisational dance group.

Sally Cook had blond hair, blue eyes and an ocean deep with talent. When she was much younger she danced with the New York City Ballet. She worked on Broadway in the 'Sound of Music'. Sally was an optimist, full of energy. She taught me to take a shot of whisky before I step in the limelight to dance.

Nicole came from France, very athletic and enthusiastic. Two decades later we met again. Nicole shyly told me at the time she believed I was upset at her because she liked to get high on pot, I had said I considered this 'unprofessional'. How curious, I thought. If true that was the pot calling the kettle black. What was I thinking? I remembered her differently. I envied her free spirit. I wanted to live her life.

Sue Smith was wild looking and very beautiful. She had studied at LaGuardia High School of Performing Arts and Julliard. She was fascinated by the Graham style because she too held a passion for dramatic expressions. After a back injury, she became a dance therapist. Besides dance we shared a yearning for a spiritual path.

Tysan was two years old when I worked with these exceptional women. I would read Dr. Seuss books to Tysan during the rehearsal breaks. One day I found an unusual hat in a flea market. I started to wear the hat while dancing. I would glide and spin, hop and leap, skip and stomp like a child. Then I would turn and ask, "Do you like my hat?" "No. We do not like your hat," three women plus a two year old would shout back at me.

Martin and I considered ourselves avant-garde by eating natural and uncooked food. We hiked in the woods wearing non-synthetic clothing. We fancied ourselves pure spirits.

When Martin and I were at Goddard, we had created a project, 'Martin and Yung Yung in Concert'. We coached four other college friends in Primal Therapy and Theater Encounter. I taught them the Chinese silk-ribbon dance. It was the story of a Chinese empress, Chang Er. How she flew to the moon to escape her cruel husband's thirst for wars. She later taught her descendant, another emperor, Tang Ming Huang to dance, to fly through ribbons. And silk fascinated me. I watched silk flow through air, dance in free style patterns. I would love to be as soft and free as silk.

In the next few months Brad eventually took over our business. Martin watched his guru turn all too human, greedy and hungry for power. Was this part of Martin's enlightenment?

◆   ◆   ◆

We were back and forth from Woodstock to his parents' house at Harrison, NY. Where the Lerners had parties. Friends debated and argued politics amid the rich smell of food and good wine. Since we had become vegans of course we only inhaled the aromas.

At one party Judy had invited Yuan Chi, a Chinese woman, to be the honored guest. Yuan Chi and her husband Paul were fresh from China. Paul was an American working there as a specialist on Chinese-American relationships. Yuan Chi was his assistant. Paul looked fiftyish his wife seemed to be in her early thirties. Martin's parents and their friends asked a million questions. Yuan Chi answered in a proper, diplomatic manner. She reminded me of the typical Chinese Communist profile in the Taiwanese propaganda papers. She spoke fluent English, clear and cold. She enunciated her words, syllable by syllable to emphasize her ideas. At one point she popped her eyes, opened her mouth wide and told everyone that the revolution was necessary even if there was blood to be sacrificed.

Taiwan had long withdrawn from the United Nations. I was very much cut off from what was happening there. I was cut off from my Chinese heritage. My parents were in the process of coming to America. Bits and pieces of information had been received from the Mainland. We knew Father's second uncle was executed, one of his sons jumped off the roof of a building at the age of seventeen, or was he pushed by a red guard? Mother's cousin was sent to a labor camp for over twenty years, so was Father's aunt. Another cousin was shot and the family charged two dollars for the bullet. 'Blood to be sacrificed.' Horror stories sprang out of Chinese communities about the Cultural Revolution. But Chairman Mao had wowed Martin's family.

When there was a lull, I gathered some courage to ask Yuan Chi. I spoke in Mandarin, "Do you really think it's worth the bloodshed for the cause of a revolution?"

Yuan Chi did not answer me. I forced my words out, "How can any thing be worth the suffering of people? How can we allow the government to close the door and beat its citizens like dogs?"

Yuan Chi gave me a painful look. I knew she heard me. Maybe I had touched her heart? Then someone loudly asked another question. Yuan Chi returned to her propaganda explaining how China was great. I became invisible again. What is the truth about China I wondered? I had been scared to speak up. Judy had once said she would not associate with any one who had opposing political agendas. Was I in such need of approval?

The guests left one by one. Martin and I were alone in the living room. Tysan had fallen asleep on the couch.

"I don't belong to your family," I murmured to Martin. "What?" Martin seemed high from the party. "Nothing," I replied, and buried the words down my throat.

Eleven

I had continued to search for help after Tysan was born. Through the grapevine I found a woman therapist who was highly recommended by the locals. I met her in her apartment/office in the center of Woodstock town. She had me hit pillows and demanded I scream out my anger. At the time I felt calm. I had nothing to be angry about. I merely wished to continue delving into my psyche. She would scream at me. I told her I was going to quit therapy. She told me I had not worked out my sexual frustration. I left anyway. I had no idea what she was talking about.

One day Tysan and I were busy bagging raisins at Nature's Pantry when an angry and flustered Martin burst in the store. "What happened?"

"You won't believe this," he was out of breath, "But I just saw John on the street. I asked about the thou he owed me. Guess what? He hit me!"

I remembered the night after Brad's evening's lecture when Martin came home all excited about John. How smart he was, a talented a singer he had appeared in the film version of 'Hair'. Martin was impressed John had received ten thousand dollars for one day's work. He especially liked how John enquired about 'life' in sessions with the guru. He had finally met someone close up who had touched a glimpse of stardom. Soon Martin arranged for John to work with me. He sang and danced in our living room. Then early one morning John showed up on our doorstep. He was saddled down with a backpack, two suitcases, and a few shopping bags. His newly-wed wife had kicked him out. Martin enthusiastically took him in. He stayed with us for several weeks. Before John left he persuaded Martin to loan him a thousand dollars. I was amazed. I thought we had no cash. I had been working extra jobs cleaning houses. Six months passed since John left our house. Martin continued to see him at Brad's evening lectures. Money was never mentioned.

I did not know if I should be angry with Martin or laugh at him. Looking at his half swollen face, I said, "It's a fair exchange. You loved his fame and he loved your money."

The store was failing. Martin's relationship with his father had deteriorated. I was cut off from their drama. The dancing and the music sustained my spirits. That and my love for Tysan, who was rapidly becoming my favorite student.

Martin continued to follow the guru. One evening, a Chinese man showed up. He had a huge following in Tai Chi Chuan and Tao philosophy. Martin started to interact with this man. He asked many questions about the principles of Tai Chi and the concept of Tao. After the Chinese master left, the Brad turned to Martin and said it would be good-bye if Martin responded this way to another guest. Martin was shocked.

I returned to a familiar theme for a new dance, 'Flight to the Moon' was the name later to be revised. I created the first version of this dance in Woodstock. The musicians who participated in the process of rehearsals and performances were talented. Michael White and his rock group played a traditional style of Woodstock Rock and folk songs. Beth McLaughlin played Jazz violin with a classical touch. Many of the local artists helped with our stage set. Soon the women's drumming group joined us. We rented the Byrdcliffe Theater, a summer stock venue originally founded by Joanne Woodward. We were professionals now. Martin was so inspired he wanted to immediately change his business. Why not manage a dance company? So much more exciting than Nature's Pantry where he had to haul bags of flour, bags of rice and bags of raisins, Where he had to answer his father's 'I tell you what to do' and his mother's nag. He believed we would be able to make a living by marketing 'Yung Yung Tsuai Dance Company'. Here we differed. I could not see the possibilities. Modern dancers were not able to support themselves, how was I, an unknown, going to support a family of three? Shadows from my professional past began to inhabit the base of my spine. Martin had such a big vision and inspirational enthusiasm, yet he could not see me. I tried to tell him, "no." My 'no' was not strong enough. Motivated by the dance troupe idea and disillusioned by his guru Martin sold Nature's Pantry.

We moved temporarily to Martin's parents' house in Harrison. Judy was irritated by Martin and frequently screamed at him. One night they had a huge yelling fight and we moved out in an old beaten up red Chevrolet convertible jam packed with our suitcases, blankets, and four year old Tysan. Luckily, we found an apartment.

Roosevelt Island was located in the middle of the East River between Manhattan and Queens. On Second Avenue and Fifty-Ninth Street a bright orange tram trolley shuttled people over the East river. Boats, tugboats and sometimes ships floated through the river and glided under the Fifty-ninth street Bridge. The apartment buildings were built in the Seventies, with cement sidings and large glass windows. On the North tip of the island, there was an old castle surrounded by a few ruins and a defunct garden. I was told the island had been a prison and the castle a psychiatric hospital. We could see sections of big ships drift across our living room window. Very often I thought it was a hallucination.

Martin was then convinced I could make money and support the family by dancing. We founded the Yung Yung Tsuai Dance Company. I returned to teach at the Graham School for cash flow. Martin managed our dance company hoping to hit stardom. In reality I taught dance at various schools and he worked for a temping agency. But we persevered with our company.

◆   ◆   ◆

Dancers learn to use their bodies as instruments. We push to the limit of our physical capacity. If we break through the barrier of physical limitation, there is a chance to glimpse the enormous unknown energy locked within our bodies. Martha Graham created a technique, which I believe is more difficult than any other dance form. To dance her technique the dancers must keep muscles strong and limber at the same time. The Graham technique helps dancers break through limitations. In general it is a painful methodology. What is fascinating is how the dancers sustain the hardship of her technique, addicted to the movements once they understand the possibilities.

I came to Martha's life when she was declining. Pearl Lang, the great dancer, said no one had Martha's grace and charisma. When Martha was fifty years old she was able to do a full evening's work like Dame Margot Fonteyn.

Maybe I was not as talented as I was told in my childhood. I knew I could not devote a full heart to Martha. We had different sensibilities. Outwardly, I kept up with her technique classes. Later, I would become a faithful dance teacher at her school. Inwardly, I had a debate going for three decades. Why was I dancing? The debate exhausted me and prevented me from whole-heartedly pursuing a career with the Martha Graham Company. Each time I had a chance to join her dance company, I withdrew.

Martha was a master of dance. I admired her. I was devoted to her. But something pulled me back, withheld my full commitment to her. She had the ability to manifest the human psyche through movement. To learn to execute those movements could help expose emotional traumas. I had a problem with publicly glorifying inner darkness. I was motivated to bring balance to the world. Madness won't do. I had identified with Martha's works and appreciated her contributions to the dance world. And I saw her darkness disguised by the beauty of a stage.

Another paradox: I remained faithful to her technique, yet not able to bring myself to commit to her performances. There was a profound conceptual split between us. Her father had been an early exponent of psychiatry. He worked in what were then called Insane Asylums. He explained to Martha how he diagnosed the unbalanced emotions by observing an individual's body movements as well as facial expressions. He told her he observed four legged animals the same way.

I had often wondered if Monica Beerle's fate was a result of the Graham approach: insanity as art? Monica came from Switzerland to study at the Graham school during the Eighties. She was tall, slim and lighthearted. Full of energy with a cocky smile, Monica danced enthusiastically. Martha was teaching, empowering us in her temple of dance. I too was full of aspiration and I lived solely for achievement. I had just begun to teach. My notion about dance had been my highest goal. In one of the composition classes, I watched Monica hold her hands over her throat in an attempt to separate her head from her body. She jerked her movement in such a way I thought it was disgraceful. I was so judgmental. Monica was dancing in an overly dramatic way swinging her head in different directions. From my limited view I did not see her true intention: Monica was frantically crying for help through improvisational movement.

Thousands of dancers came to New York City each year. Foreign students floated through the dance schools: Martha Graham School, Alvin Ailey School, Merce Cuningham Studio or New York City Ballet, Joffery Ballet and Feld Ballet. With little exception no one cared about where they came from or where they were going. Friends and families lost track. We did not know who Monica really was or how she lived. Students partied with her. They had lunch and drank coffee together, but this concern went no further. Everyone was busy. When Monica disappeared for a couple of months, no one asked about her. The news came from the newspaper: 'The man whose nickname was Birdman murdered a Martha Graham dance student.' Daniel Rakowitz originally from Texas was a regular at Thompson Square Park, a pet rooster perched on his shoulder. Apparently, Monica and Daniel shared an apartment together. One day, a neighbor walked into their apartment and discovered Monica's head cooking in a soup pot. The neighbor freaked out and did not report it to the police for a week. When the police broke in, they found bits and pieces of Monica everywhere. The Birdman had killed, cooked and ate her. He also distributed 'Monica soup' to the homeless people in Thompson Square Park. Her bones had been stored in a locker at Grand Central Station.

Mother had written me about her desire to leave Taiwan. She told me it was getting bad in Taiwan, unsafe for the Mandarins. She told me one night a taxi driver drove four Mandarin women to a graveyard after their Mahjong game. The taxi driver forced them to sing all night long in front of a tomb. Mother was terrified by this incident. Compare to New York City it seemed comical.

When the horror of Monica's fate reached the school, the student body broke down. Dance schools throughout the city hired full time counselors for their students. Many students who had left home to come to the big city chasing the dream of becoming professional dancers revealed their heart-broken stories. As a result the position of a Dean of Students was created to oversee the students' needs. Emergency funds were set up for students who were going through hardships.

Later, I speculated if I had detected Monica's suffering in the improvisation class, as some of my teachers had done with me. Would it have made a difference? Conditions for dance students had improved. Nevertheless achievement remained the central focus: either you are a star in the teachers' eyes, on the way to a major dance company, or you are nothing, a failure.

I was happy to see Pearl Lang at the Graham School. Everything was warmer with her presence especially as Martha was becoming so fragile. Pearl needed a little girl for her company tour to Montreal, Canada. The school recommended Tysan who was proving to be a natural born dancer with talent and beauty. Pearl hired me as well. We rehearsed with Pearl for over a month. She would buy an ice cream cone for Tysan after every rehearsal. During one rehearsal Pearl yelled at Tysan, "8 counts. 8 counts … your hands reach up, to the top of your head." Tysan stopped, "But you told me its 10 counts." The dancers laughed. It took a seven-year-old to talkback to Pearl.

I worked with Pearl Lang on and off after the Montreal tour. I became a dancer in her company, a stand in for her and a rehearsal director. I was indebted to Pearl for the many suggestions she gave me in teaching the Graham technique. One day we were in the faculty room discussing technique. I asked her how to instruct my students about one particular dance movement called "tilts". She said, "It's all up on one hip." She patted her hip and lifted her spine. Then an overwhelming sadness enwrapped her. She said, "Twenty-five years of lifting up this hip and now I do not have a hip. I have a replacement."

Pearl had worked hard to dedicate her entire life to the dancer's world. But her fame could not mend her frustration and sadness. She had tried to compete with Martha Graham and was unable to break through the web Martha had created.

I saw Bill Carter again at the studio. I had forgotten how handsome he was. It was wonderful to see him. We reminisced how he had invited me to luncheon when I first came to New York. I remarked it must have been a lonely meal for him as I did not speak much English. Bill had been Pearl's professional partner throughout their careers. I mentioned to Pearl how he was the person who introduced me to Martha in Taipei. Pearl nodded, "Bill would give the shirt off his back. He's generous in so many ways." I was lucky to dance with William for one of Pearl's film projects. We danced through wind, water, and sun. Two white lilies flying across the stage. Our chemistry was flawless. Afterward, I went back to William's dressing room. I wanted to present him with a piece of peach jade. He said the jade would be his good luck charm forever more. But it was not powerful enough for this lifetime. Sadly William passed away in 1985 but he continued to live in my heart.

People would ask what it is like to work with Martha or Pearl. They wanted gossip or some fantasy about the celebrity. I could never understand this. I who had lived through this dilemma perceived Martha and Pearl as persons with inner struggles, inferiorities, always fighting unresolved issues.

My new responsibilities felt like a trap. I was not at peace. It was in the works for my family to emigrate. We had found a place for them in New Rochelle. Martin and I were in family therapy. It was not helping me. Martin could not shake his neurotic focus on his parents while I remained traumatized by my childhood. Nothing had budged in our habitual pattern department. Meanwhile, I seemed to be shouldering multiple careers. Maybe I had more in common with Judy Garland than I thought. She kept performing until she dropped dead.

◆   ◆   ◆

"Your mother is Jewish. I'm Chinese. She lives in a big house in Westchester. I struggle for a few hundred dollars a week. She is "Judy Lerner" and I'm nobody. She is the best friend of Bella Abzug and William Kunstler. She knows Shirley McLain, Jane Fonda and many other celebrities. She is a feminist, a leader in the Anti-Vietnam peace movement. She has two master degrees. She is glamorous and gives great parties with her friends who talk about politics. She went to North Vietnam and China in the early Seventies."
I reminded Martin. "I come from the small island of Taiwan. My father worked for the South African government and fled China while China had glorious Communist Revolutions. Your mother is out spoken. She has many

opinions. She is rich and the center of attention. I can barely get myself together."

Martin was next to me in our bed. I could tell he did not understand. He was unable to hear me. He turned to his side and curled up in a fetus position.

I attempted to engage Martin's attention. I needed him to understand.

"I'm three years older than you. Don't try to make me your mother. I can't be your mother. I won't be able to compete with your mother. She is five feet and nine inches tall. I'm five feet. I don't feel like a mother, let alone your mother. You see, I grew up slowly, without a mother's warm embracing arms. Can someone as small as me be your mother? I can see how you try to make me fit your ideal image; how you try to manipulate me as your mother; how you push and persist I should care for you. It's just that I never grew up. We both are immature. It may sound stupid and cliché', but it's true." Martin's eyes told me he thought I was babbling.

"You know how I cry in my heart. Perhaps I can run away; perhaps I can pretend I don't love you at all, perhaps I can make myself not care. I simply don't want you to look at me and see your mother. Your mother is so glamorous and beautiful. I'm nothing. Yes! My grandma used to call me ugly duckling. She told me I could never compare with my cousin, who was the swan, the beauty. Her father was the high official under Chiang Kai-shek's government. I'm so completely screwed up I can't be your mother. I can't give you what you want. I can't take care of you.

"Love me? Love me not? This is a one-way conversation. Do we really talk to each other? What's going on in each of our heads? Love me? Love me not? Love me? But if we do commit to each other with our love, then what is going to happen to our individual dreams? Perhaps I'm too vulnerable for you; perhaps I'm too weak in your parents' eyes; perhaps I'm too dull and tired to ask for love from you; perhaps I'm too inadequate to be a mother. I'm not ready to grow up, not yet.

"In the first year of my junior high, I had to go to the bathroom for the entire evening from five to ten. I was scared of the dark. I could not go to the bathroom. The bathrooms smelled like death was crawling inside the little potholes. I really thought some kind of evil ghosts curled up in those smelly holes. So I held everything in. I had to take two buses for the one and half-hour trip back home. Then I walked in a dark alley alone for another twenty minutes, I rang the bell. Mother opened the door. She saw I was standing in a puddle. I'd peed in my skirt unable to hold it in any longer. I never thought to squat in the alley. Mother became so angry she knocked me down with her

fists. No! No! Martin, I won't be your mother. I don't trust my impulses. I already have a daughter. As your wife, I want to love you, but I can't take your mother's place. I see you snoring. I want to run away. Love me? Love me not? Don't ignore me.

"I don't have much energy to focus on world affairs. You are a thirty-one year old boy and I am a thirty-four year old girl. We have been married for ten years and now I feel that you want me to be responsible for your life. It hurts because deep down we are so similar. We both have not grown up, we are lost in a 'grown-up's world, pretending to play the grown ups games. Please look at me."

I yearned for Martin to see me. He turned over.

"Perhaps we need to run away from each other. We need to run in different directions, look for security blankets somewhere else. Perhaps, we need different caves to hide in. Why do you yearn for your mommy? Why do you pull my legs when you yearn for your mommy? I can't feel my own mother."

Martin stretched his lean strong arms over his head.

"Love me? Love me not? I can't be your mother, but I do want you to love me …"

I moved closer to him, stretching my short muscles towards him. Martin and I embraced each other into the dark night.

◆   ◆   ◆

Martin's father grew up on the lower eastside of Manhattan. His father Sam came from Poland at the age of sixteen. When he arrived at Ellis Island, the immigration officer gave him a surname "Lerner" as a learned scholar. Sam was good with his hands, especially sewing. He started to sew girdles for women but made more money by sewing men's suits for Jewish gangsters. He was able to bring his entire family over to work in his sewing business. He opened a women's clothing and under garment store on Fordham Road in the Bronx. He named his store "Mary Lerner" after his wife. For decades this became a successful retail chain.

Sam and Mary had a daughter and a son. After their daughter died of pneumonia at the age of eighteen they showered their love on Irving, their son. Irving married young. Unfortunately, the Second World War began and he went into the Navy right after his daughter was born. Irving spent seven years fighting Japanese soldiers in the South Pacific. His wife suffered a depression while he was gone. She never quite recovered. When Irving returned home they divorced. He went to work for his father where he eventually met Judy who was just another employee at the Mary Lerner store.

Martin's grandma came from Russia. She lost her first husband in a Tuberculosis epidemic. They had two children. She put their infant daughter, Tillie in an orphanage to survive the poverty. She struggled to make a living for herself and her older son Mark. Then she met Judy's father. A year later they married. Father Kohler had immigrated to the United States many years before. He left his family in Austria who for generations had been farmers. Tragically, the Nazis were to kill all of them. Mrs. Kohler was able to bring Tillie back home to start a new life. There were to be two more children, Kivy and Judy. The family struggled for sheer survival in a Bronx Jewish settlement. When Judy became a young woman she entered Hunter College to be a teacher. She perceived herself as smart, intellectual and progressive. It was at Hunter College that she became politically active, passing out fliers, picketing on sidewalks, and speaking up at political meetings. She thrived at rallies. She joined the women's movement and considered herself left wing. Her mother was a simple peasant who hated the Russian Communists, but Judy's aunt Estee had been a Russian Revolutionary who carried a rifle and fought in the Russian Revolution. Judy inherited her aunt's spirit and believed she could change the world.

Irving and Judy found a common ground. They were both social activists. Even though Irving had become a successful businessman through the expansion of his father's business, managing six or seven stores in the Bronx, White Plains and Long Island did not stop him from being politically active. And having three children, Martin, David and Mary Beth did not bind them home either. They immersed themselves in civil rights.

Martin followed his parents' footsteps. He helped to publish a school paper 'Free Press' in his last year of high school. Irving constantly interfered. Not only his son was fighting a cause he approved of, but Martin provided an open door for Irving's unfulfilled dream of becoming a writer. Irving had gone to UCLA to study English Literature. He had aspired to be a writer but his dream was crushed by the Second World War. By the end of Martin's school year, students from the 'Free Press' took over the school to protest the war. Martin's parents were thrilled. Suddenly, Martin withdrew; it was no longer his fight but his father's. After he graduated from high school, Martin went to Europe. He lived there for a year and half trying to find his own strength. He refused to be supported by his parents. He told me he was exuberant when he tore his father's check up in France. Instead, he stomped grapes for a French vineyard, impersonated a British country boy to work for an Arabian construction company to move stones, tended cows and roamed about an Israeli Kibbutz. After he returned to America he did not go back home. He went to San Francisco to meet a few of his schoolmates. He stayed in a Hippie 'commune', a militant gay women's radical group lived next door. The women had a closet full of rifles. He did not feel it was his war, but women's liberation was not an unfamiliar idea to him. However a more peaceful approach suited him. He soon left the house to learn Zen meditation. When he experienced a bad acid trip he returned east to seek therapy. He said he believed he had found home when he met me.

The womb of a non-English speaking tiny Chinese girl with crooked eyeglasses who could dance.

◆　　◆　　◆

The Yung Yung Tsuai Dance Company was chosen to perform for the Riverside Church Dance Festival. For a new program I revived 'Flight to the Moon' (the ribbon dance) now included one male and three female dancers. For the process of making the costumes I was able to research at the Museum of Natural History. I collected colorful photo slides of space shots. I had my costume designer tie dye the white silk costumes and ribbons in outer-space psychedelic multi-colors. In the middle of the dance, the music went off. The dancers moved to silence while the colors created an effect of flying in outer space. I was soon offered a scholarship to attend a choreography workshop in Texas. I took the opportunity. Florence Warren was in charge of the workshop. She was an elegant French woman in her Sixties. She was full of energy, ideas and encouragement. We were given assignments to work with young pre-professional dancers in the afternoon and expected to produce their work at night. It was a highly demanding environment that was equally supportive and professional.

I wanted to create a dance based on the character of Lady MacBeth for a young dancer. I began to talk her through the movements, step by step. The young musician who created a score for the dance was so taken by my repetitive murmuring in the dancer's ear he decided to record me. My voice? I sound like a duck. I went directly to Florence to protest. She encouraged me to see the possibilities. I finally gave in. That night I watched Lady MacBeth dance to my murmuring sounds. It worked! One small step away from my rigidity. Years later, I received a grant from the New York State Council on the Arts to create another dance for the Asian American Dance Theater. I used the same format but chose to create a different subject. I wanted to tell the story of a repressed Chinese woman. I decided to create a character similar to my grandma, a woman who embroidered, who had bound feet, and had been married off. I called the dance 'Memoir'. This dance received great reviews and won many awards. This happened as I learned to draw on my psychological pain. Later, my daughter Tysan learned the piece and performed it throughout the United States as well as Asia.

Another dance which received equal attention was the Song of the Great Wall. It came out of the Theater Encounter workshop. I was telling a story about my father's visit back to China after forty years of exile. How he began to laugh, but the laugh sounded like crying to me. This time my stage props were no longer silk but cotton clothing for the family, porcelain wine cups to celebrate the family reunion, red ribbons to tie the family together, a string of rubber bands to separate them. A Chinese kite to fly to freedom, and black lacquered wooden sticks to fight an internal war.

Martin was convinced we could make it. He was sure we would hit stardom. This time a husband not a father was organizing my professional life.

Martin found an old Polish social club in New Rochelle, a suburb of the City. This would be our dance studio. We went about renovating the wooden floor, painted the walls and mounted the mirrors and ballet bars. To save money we immediately sublet our Roosevelt Island apartment and moved into the backroom of the dance studio. By now my family had successfully emigrated from Taiwan. The story went AnAn had finally been called up by the army for a physical examination.

"Bu De Lia La! Jia Ru AnAn Bai Tzeo Chu Dang Bing, Na Zte Mu De Lia? (Can't carry the Heaven! If AnAn is drafted, how can he survive?)" Mother had dressed him in beige Khaki pants and jacket, over a starched white shirt. At the army base he did well. He was able to answer the questions.

The medical doctor looked at him, "Who could say he is sick? He looks normal ..." before the doctor finished his sentence, AnAn was on the floor, rolling and kicking. "Bu De Lia La! Jia Ru AnAn Bai Tzeo Chu Dang Bing, Na Zte Mu De Lia? (Can't carry the Heaven! If AnAn is drafted, how can he survive?)" AnAn mimicked our parents' words in a loud raucous voice. Thus, he did not serve. The road was paved for my family to immigrate to the USA.

For years the side effect from his medication made AnAn a basket case. Once in New York with his new doctor AnAn learned control. He was able to go to work. Maybe AnAn was a simpleton but he was pure. Father said, "AnAn was a simple god from heaven before he incarnated to this world." He spoke with a swell of his chest and a bright shine in his eyes. Mother smiled, her eyes half-closed. She was patting AnAn's head.

"When I die, I'll go to Heaven and be a simple god." AnAn repeated to Father.

"Yes. I'll wait for you in Heaven. The second you pass the death door, just call my name," Father said to AnAn so warmly, his voice could melt butter.

Martin investigated every possible dance venue. He contacted a hotel in Las Vegas. I looked at his innocent, bright eyes and laughed, "Martin, Vegas show-girls are six feet tall. I'm barely five feet. Remember?" Martin had successfully booked me at the beautifully majestic Chitagua Theater in upstate New York. I performed 'Memoir'. Huai Lang Yuan and Gary Wang created a stage set with bright red and gold embroidered Chinese kimonos. Brooks Williams, the composer set a score of eerie sounds, overlapping my voice on top of the synthesized string instruments. The text was a repetitive pattern of a few statements: my grandma sat and embroidered until she was married off, her feet bound. I think of home, I think about her bound feet, I think of the old China with its embroidered lily bags.

It was an outdoor concert hall in a magnificent park. While I was dancing on stage I could see the moon shining and the stars twinkling in the sky. I was no longer in my body, controlling my muscles and mastering the steps. My vision had turned crystal clear. I felt so much bigger than the bone and flesh of my actual physical structure. I was following the pre-designed patterns of movement without effort. A gentle breeze carried my spirit. My soul merged with the stars and the moon. In this way I could witness myself dancing on stage. I experienced the divine.

Martha Graham explored the muscular manipulations of human emotions. Merce Cunningham experimented on the relationship and relativities of time and space with his life partner, the composer, John Cage. They used spontaneity to explore random chances. Balanchine, who had great knowledge of classical and contemporary music, choreographed ballets marrying to the music. I had never been a dance historian or dance scholar. My focus in dance had been scattered by chaotic living situations. I had spent a lot of time and energy confronting the challenges of a difficult childhood. My dancing skills and therapy were intertwined. Dance helped me to understand my body. The memories stored in the cells of my body gradually emerged. My choreography became rooted in the revision of my life experiences.

Tysan and I made up the eight dancers of the Yung Yung Tsuai Dance Company. Occasionally other dancers were invited to join us. But when I think of my dance troupe I think of the other six dancers who danced with us for over five years. We were a warm and talented family, each with great respect for the other. A family within a family. Which was the real family?

Martin was successful in booking our troupe. But there was not enough money. There never was. I had to come up with new choreography. It reminded me of the pressured Taiwan TV days when the studio depended on my performance and my dance creativities as well.

Here I was in the New Rochelle studio with a blank mind and the same burden of responsibility. The concert was a week away. I thought of my friend KK a dancer I had worked with at the Graham School who had died two weeks ago. He was a wonderful colleague. His death left me emotionally empty. We often enjoyed a drink in the bar next door to the Graham Studio. He told me of his ambitions. An injury had forced him to retire from dancing in the Company. But he could teach and he aspired to be a choreographer. Then he fell seriously ill. I was told he had been turned down by the hospital for lack of beds. He died at home. Fortunately, his partner stayed with him. Thinking of this loss, I became so agitated I started to twirl. Inspired, I twirled and twirled and twirled. I reached KK's world by twirling. Out of this came my dance, Emanation, set to the music by another childhood friend, Shih Chih. Whenever I perform this dance I dedicate it to KK before the audience.

◆   ◆   ◆

Martha died in 1991at age 94. Martha willed her entire possessions, including her lifetime creative work to Ron Protas who became the executive director of her company and school right after her passing. Ron had an extremely difficult time. He was round faced, wore glasses and a toupee. Ron was medium built with a nervous demeanor. He also was losing his hearing which perversely motivated him to talk obsessively. He took medicine for his nerves. At times he would flash an alluring, boyish smile.

He was theatrical with a larger than life air. He began to believe he was Martha Graham's son. Then, Martha Graham herself which explained why he began to talk and act like her.

One day I found Ron lying on the couch in the teacher's lounge. He started to sing, to charm me. I was tone deaf, so I felt I could not join in. I stood stiff as a board. He looked as if I was letting him down because I refused to play. Suspicion and fear prevented us from being at ease with one other. He must have suspected most of us saw him as a troubled person. I felt he was in trouble, even though he blamed everyone around him. He acted out his insecurity. His mind and his heart did not connect. He was not equipped for the gift Martha had willed him.

"People didn't think Martha cared. She did. It would have been nice if you reached out." He was right there. I never did. I never reached out to Pearl either beyond professional courtesy. There were many opportunities. Why did I keep a distance? Was it the burden of being famous when I was young? I did not want Martin to know I was famous in Taiwan. I did not want Martin to know I was a scholarship student at the Martha Graham School. When I saw Martha, Pearl and many other famous dancers, I did not think of their fame and glory but as individuals with struggles and pain.

I believed Martha Graham's world was not an easy environment for Ron Protas. He accused Diane Gray, the associate director of the school and the company of wanting his position. He developed hostility to other faculty members. I was caught in between. Ron tried his best to win me over. Diane had been my first Graham teacher. She taught me well and she treated me well. How could I go against her?

I became the director of the teen-age program at the Graham School. One Saturday morning I conducted an audition. Marianne Bachmann, the dean of the students and Peter Londen, the principal dancer of the Company made up the panel. There were about ninety teenagers attending on this audition. The audition was going well until Ron showed up. My heart sank. The serpent was ready to flip his tongue and slash his victim. I introduced Ron to the students before I proceeded with the audition. Every five minutes he would interrupt me. At one point he screamed. "No! Stop counting. When Martha was alive she hated dancers who counted. You must feel the rhythm."

Ron interfered, "Let's experiment with this movement..." I was dumbfounded.

The student's movements became a wave of chaos. Ron was ordering a professional demand on beginner students. The class fell apart. Ron did not give up. He talked compulsively. The class dragged on. In distress I finally ended the class.

It was the beginning of my problem with Ron. He took many meetings with me regarding the curriculum. These meetings were intense. He was full of ideas. My job was to listen to Ron. I had no idea what he was talking about, except to ask me to love him and to confide Diane did not love him. Although on the surface, we discussed dance recital programs, which were held at the end of each year. The subtext was Ron's personal torment. He was at odds with everyone. He tried to get my support. How could I help him? I had already been disillusioned by the dance world. I had witnessed so many dancer injuries, seen their pain.

During one meeting Ron said he knew I had a good heart, but heart was not what he was looking for. He wanted the program to be good.

What is good? 'Traditionally, dancers' bodies should be like musical instruments, they played to the wonder of the eyes.'

But I knew to create an image of a perfect body had destroyed so many young girls. Anorexia and bulimia were common in that effort to have a 'perfect body'. How shall we judge anyone's body? Why must we deny the dancers their natural body types? Why do we insist on believing we can mold the bodies?

I walked out of Ron's office knowing my traditional disciplines and beliefs were falling apart. Since childhood I had believed I must devote myself to the art of dance; I believed one should absolutely sacrifice oneself to the perfect image on stage; I believed dancers should be gods and goddesses and their bodies could make the necessary transformation. I believed mediocrity was a sin. Slowly through the years of therapy, another thought had strengthened in my heart and mind: There should be no sacrifice for art. No one should be allowed to mold another's body. We could teach techniques of how to use our muscles and bones, we could inspire creativity, and we could up-lift the spirit. But it would be a sin if we ever made anyone feel inadequate about what they were born with.

I knew if I quit then, I would lose everything. My entire life's work. The weekly paycheck along with my identity in the dance world would come to an end without a trace. There would be no pension or unemployment. I thought of three of my students and their fates. Their stories helped me to make a decision. When I thought of them I knew it would be the right thing to follow my heart.

Tangi was an African American scholarship student at the Graham school. She came from one of the projects in Crown Heights, Brooklyn. With a shy smile on her face, she danced faithfully in every class. She moved sensually and fluently. She was about five feet and six inches tall and weighed about one hundred and fifty pounds when she was fourteen. I told her if she was serious about dancing she needed to lose weight. Instead of breaking down crying like other students, Tangi did not compromise. She smiled, "Miss Yung Yung, I'm comfortable with my body." She swayed her hips and tilted her head as she walked away. I said nothing. I respected Tangi. She was not going to bend to the world's demand for a slim and lengthy body. Tangi held her own ground. My perception began to shift. I saw there were other ways to look at a woman's body. Tangi had put an end to the weight question that dominated my dance world. She did not show up for the scholarship audition in September 1996. Without paying much attention, I invalidated her scholarship for that year.

The following spring there was quite a commotion after a class; students were talking excitedly to one another. I was told Tangi had had a baby. She gave birth to a girl at the beginning of March. I decided to pay a visit to Tangi and her baby girl. The moment I exited the subway it seemed the entire neighborhood came out to greet me. I was rarely in this part of the city and now I was received by a few of my students with warm hearts and everlasting smiles. First they took me to visit one of Tangi's aunts and uncles. After a few words of greetings other kids showed up. The night was getting dark as were the streets, but a global smile permeated the air. Sweet smells emanated through the alleys and perfumed us with warm hearts. We entered another building and now there were ten or more teenagers. I was introduced to another uncle and aunt. They directed me to a room at the end of a long hallway where Tangi was sitting on the edge of the bed holding a tiny baby wrapped in a pink and blue blanket. She looked up and smiled, "This is my baby, Miss Yung Yung." Looking at Tangi's fifteen-year-old face my self-importance slipped under my thighs. I did not know if I should feel joy for her or worry. She looked content and happy. I did not dare to ask where her parents were. How she was going to support her child? I did not dare touch the reality. What was the reality? I never saw Tangi and her baby again, except in my heart. I wished I knew how her life turned out. I did not extend myself. How could I ever demand anything from those kids? How could I ever tell them if they danced well or not?

Shirlee was sixteen when she dropped out of the program. Shirlee's family came from Haiti. Shirlee had been an excellent scholarship student for four years. Thin, tall and muscular, Shirlee danced gracefully and intelligently. She was always very quiet and worked hard in class. With her dark hair neatly parted in the center, she cast her eyes down as if she was looking within her soul while she moved vigorously with strong rhythm. Shirlee suddenly disappeared about the same time Tangi had her baby. I kept asking Shirlee's friends. Where is she? Then I learned the sad truth. "Shirlee's mother died of AIDS two months ago, and her father threw her out on streets," her friends said. "Shirlee wouldn't talk. She clamed up kept everything inside." "Shirlee's proud. She never jives." "We always looked up to her. She was our model, the way she could dance."

One day Shirlee did show up in school. After the class I walked her to the subway. 'Are you Okay?" She nodded her head. "If you need anything, let me know" She nodded her head. "Do you have any place to stay?" She nodded her head. We said good-bye. It was the last time I saw her.

Most of the teen-agers lived in the city with their families and friends. They would attend various performing arts high schools and take private dance classes after regular school hours. Their goal was to become professional dancers. They studied hard and were physically well trained. However, most of the better dance schools were made up of professional trainee programs, which were designed for adult, international students. I also taught in the Graham professional division. Many of my students were already professionals in their native country. They lived poorly without much support.

I had met an African dancer named Jay Jay who in his country was the chief of the village. He told me dancers from his village had first to be initiated by their gods to do certain dances, such as "purifying the air" and "raising the dead". Otherwise they could become physically injured. And I believed him.

I learned to dance, sing, to play musical instruments, to tell stories, to make stage sets, and to dress up in costumes. But I knew I was living far from the gods. I did not realize how blindfolded I was, without any initiations from higher beings. Some of us do not think higher energies exist. We believe in entertainments.

I learned celebrity was fueled by the profits it gendered. Mediocrity could rise to stardom. In Martha Graham's case she was a genuine talent. As Agnes De Mille believed she was a genius. And Martha was worshipped by elite during her lifetime yet she died financially poor.

When it came to the point of choosing between a good heart and being on stage, as Ron Protas had indicated to me, I resigned from my teaching job at the Graham School. I quit. I would try to devote myself with a good heart to my dance company.

Twelve

For the next two years we lived illegally in the backroom of the dance studio without hot water, kitchen and shower. When we needed to bath we walked two blocks to my parents' house, if we needed a hot meal we walked two blocks to my parents' house. After school, Tysan would take a long way around the block to avoid being seen by her schoolmates. She feared they would think we were squatters.

There was nearly a month open before the dance company scheduled to tour. Father presented an opportunity for me to take a brief respite from my responsibility. Throughout the years he had expressed a yearning to go 'home' to China. He continued to talk about his childhood, his parents, his friends, his house in Wuhu, the family roots. Somehow he found a moment and money to fulfill his lifelong dream. Father invited me to join the family on this historical visit. 'Forty years of exile'. Ping had been living in Shanghai. I would like to see 'little fatty hand'. So I agreed to join the family's ten-day adventure.

The name Tsuai means 'people in a village who live under a mountain'. There is a Chinese poem: "Beyond the world, a Peach Village". The author took a boat ride and discovered a village under a mountain where peach trees bloomed year around. People were kind and warm hearted. They showed love and respect for one another. They had touched his spirit and heart. However, when the author tried to look for them the second time, he could no longer find a trace of their shadows. Would this be our experience?

The trip was under two weeks. Martin agreed it would be a good break for me. We were to visit Father's old home where the Tsuai family lived for thousands years before they moved to Wuhu City two hundred years ago. The village is called Tai Ping Village, the ultimate Peaceful Village, under the Yellow Mountain in Anhui Province.

On June 4th 1987, thousands of Chinese students and labor workers demonstrated in front of Tiananmen Square in Beijing and the government armies marched into the city and massacred many of them. The Chinese government would deny the event. Several months later, on October 11th 1987, we arrived in

Shanghai for our visit. Soldiers were everywhere with their machine guns and military tanks.

Our eight suitcases were stuffed. Mother insisted on filling six of them with second hand clothes. It was an unspoken rule: if any overseas Chinese went to China they must bring bags full of used clothes, plus a television set, a refrigerator, a juice blender, a toaster oven and many other appliances as gifts for their relatives in China. There was a saying at the time: San da jian wu shia jian (three large ones and five small ones) is a must. We were told to purchase all electronic merchandise through a Chinese shop in Hong Kong and give the receipts to whomever we choose to give the gift to. They could then exchange the receipts for merchant goods from the local government bureau. It was a way for the Chinese government to make money through overseas relatives. Mother had engrained the need for these offerings. She explained, "My brother Kang-Shing has one son and two daughters. My cousin Kang-Yee was like a brother to me and he has a son. I have never met my niece Shiao-Heng, but she is my beloved aunt's daughter and she also has a son. I have to bring some old clothes for all of them and then there are your father's aunts, uncles and cousins. I heard the rumor saying that an old soldier went back home to visit from Taiwan and did not bring enough clothes with him. His relatives stripped him naked with only a pair of underwear left."

I had envisioned waves of people, many of them relatives, wearing dark blue Mao jackets and hats. Another image was of naked people in a stark land, crouching down on a famished earth stuffing tree bark to their mouths. The Communist party members wore ox horns and horse faces and cracked whips behind the skinny people whose ribcages stuck out in torment. (This image had been drilled into my mind by Taiwanese propaganda since childhood.)

To my surprise, when I stepped out of the Shanghai airport, I saw throngs of people, bustling about in many colorful dresses and suits. The Autumn Tiger (Chinese expression of Indian summer) also chose to visit Shanghai at the same time we arrived, making the air hot and humid. I saw sweat dripping from tanned muscles; I smelled tobacco mixing with perfumes and colognes from rich business men and women; I sensed expansion and booming economics, generated by individual enterprise; I heard noise, and more noise every where, car horns, pedestrians shouting, loud speakers blasting pop music and Chinese propaganda announcements coming from storefronts, airports, train stations and restaurants.

"Pa! Ma! Here! Here!" Ping fluttered around by the airport waiting area behind the rope line. With his arms high up waving, he caught our attention.

The whole Tsuai family marched in, displaying our eight huge suitcases in hand, and so we entered Shanghai, where my father spent most of his youth. At last authentic Chinese people. Tears gathered around the corners of my eyes, I was thrilled.

After we settled in our hotel, our relatives clustered in groups to greet us. They had black straight hair and slanted eyes. Their skins were brownish yellow. Every man smoked while the women talked loudly. I was shocked to realize my own Chinese-ness, so well hidden from myself.

When Tysan was two years old, I took her to Chinatown, NY. It was her first experience outside of Woodstock. After walking around visiting many of the shops, markets and restaurants, she pulled at me with her tiny hand. I lowered my head and she asked quietly, "How come all these people look like you?"

I'd turned American in my relative's eyes. I thought how woeful. I spoke broken English and my Chinese seemed to get worse every day. I was no longer Chinese and I was not an American either. When my relatives greeted me, I could not distinguish who was who.

An old woman entered the hotel room. She carried herself straight and dignified. She reminded me of my grandma. With the same white hair combed neatly into a tight bun behind her head, she looked as sharp as she looked ancient, with Grandma's thin and angled face. The high cheekbones wrinkled with deep lines. She smiled in a stylish fashion, the familiar dark brown eyes deeply set. She spoke old Chinese wisdom through her eyes. Yet, she was bittersweet. "Where is Yung Yung? Is this my grandniece Yung Yung?" she demanded attention.

"Yung Yung! Pay your grandaunt Fu-Lian respect and bow to her," my father commanded.

"Grandaunt Fu-Lian!" I called her name in a ritual and gave her a deep bow.

"No! No! No! I should bow to you. I am so deeply in debt to what you did for me. If you did not write the letter for me in 1980 and send me money, I wouldn't be here today," she started to cry.

Grandaunt Fu-Lian was sent to a Labor Camp for over twenty years in the Fifties. When she was arrested, she had been married for only a month. Now she was an old woman. Her husband refused to accept her back. She was so poor; she had no means of support. She needed a letter written by an overseas relative, so she would be able to receive a pension. She wrote to my father who had given her my address in America. I was afraid the letter from Mainland China to Taiwan would endanger Father politically in Taiwan, so I wrote her directly, an official type letter, along with a check.

"I was never interested in politics!" she was bitter, "I was a music teacher. We knew nothing about politics. Our principle received a quota. Words circled around the school we needed three people to volunteer as anti-Communist. We drew the straws. I picked up the short straw. I was told that all I had to do was stand on stage and be criticized. We were promised no harm. It was a show for the Communist party. I was even tickled. Who could suspect that after the show military police would march in and arrest us."

My grandaunt was a tiny woman. When she smiled, her white teeth and high cheekbones formed a warm circle on her face. There was a loving glow radiating behind the bitterness.

"I met our principle the other day," she said. "I walked right by him. He looked as if he wanted to apologize, but it was my entire life! If Yung Yung did not send the letter, I would be dead on the street."

Out of nowhere Father roared with laughter. He said mockingly, "This is serious! If I hadn't taken my family out of this country, Yung Yung would be dead on the street!"

We were startled by Father's inappropriate behavior but said nothing.

Great-aunt shook her chopsticks in the air during a meal course. Moving her toothless mouth in great difficulties, great-aunt said, "He was a beauty, and very feminine. I still remember his big opening night. I went to see his performance. I was given away to a relative when we were young, but we kept in touch. He invited me with great enthusiasm. He looked stunning, with his beautiful Chinese opera make-up and costumes. But your grandma marched onto the stage and dragged him off stage. The audience laughed and applauded. What a shame! They were only seventeen years old. Your father was just born. She made a scene and humiliated him. Then I saw him on the street corner. He was wearing the same costumes but his hairpiece was off. I started to cry. I heard he left home that night ..."

Another inappropriate situation happened again at Wuhu City. Mother met her father after forty years of separation. A toothless old man with a balding head. He seemed to be very alert, but there was no affection between them. They were polite strangers. We sat at a banquet table, staring at each other. Then, again Father suddenly laughed so loud, it sounded like sobs. He complained, "When we're in Taiwan, we're outsiders. They call us Mandarin! When we're in America, we're foreigners. Now, we're home, and they want to charge us triple of the price of every thing because we're considered 'American, the foreign ghosts!'"

I understood these outbursts. It was about money. I was surprised Mother joined father, "Why should I come back? They want me to give them money and gifts. They even faked mother's graveyard to cheat more money out of me. They told me they needed to fix the gravestone. She had no grave and her ashes had been scattered over a vegetable garden!" We finished our banquet meal in silence. That was the last time she saw her father. He died a year later.

That night as I fell asleep I thought these are actions of people under tyranny, robbed of identity, their souls left to beg. This behavior is not who they are. An entire village with my surname Tsuai. Everyone a relative yet I could not relate to them.

◆   ◆   ◆

After China I returned to Martin who was chomping at the bit, impatient for me to take the company on the road. Once again he was hoping for profits. Once again I tried to communicate dance companies do not make profit. This time when the tour finished Martin announced we were without any cash flow. This meant we had to give up the studio. We could not move back to Roosevelt Island as the apartment was sublet. What was left for our little family but to seek shelter at the Lerner family house in Harrison? My stomach churned at the thought but there was no alternative. So we entered Martin's family hell-realm again. And then I was pregnant.

We did not have to be thrown out of your parents' house after your mom started to scream at you, but we were. I was a forty-year old woman when I was pregnant with our second child. You were thirty-seven. We sat in your parents' living room being lectured by your parents about how wrong it would be for me not to have an abortion. "Your child will be raised on welfare," your father said. "A welfare child will be so damaged. It will be a disgrace." We sat there and listened. We nodded our heads. "It's your body," your mother said. "You don't have to keep this child. You have a choice, a woman's choice." I said nothing. Did they know I had two abortions before? Was I so foolish I did not know about my own body? I was being told I was unable to bring up another child. Martin, you sat there and let your parents go on talking. Why? You insisted to manage my dance company despite my strong objections. So, we were poor. But why did you have to ask money from your parents? I knew your father was very sick. He was dying of cancer. But why did he become so intensely involved with our marriage and our affairs? Why would he not let go and leave me be when he found out I was pregnant? Is it because he gave us money? Is it because you asked money from your parents? Martin, take the money and shove it up to your ass. I am going away!

I had been living in a glass box trying to reach out to Martin. I wanted to crush the glass to smithereens. I could not forgive Martin's father's insistence on an abortion. It was not his business. Martin could not tell his father to butt out. He could not! He was the first-born. He was the prince married to an ugly duckling from Taiwan who could not take care of herself.

I was not of the generation of women who had to push a hanger in the womb or secretly visit a witch hidden in the outskirts of a village. I did not have to live with shame. I was not doing anything illegal. I was not living in rural China where women were held down with ropes, their wombs opened to have a five months old fetus taken out. Their babies killed. I did not feel horrified because I needed an abortion. Modern technology helped me avoid physical suffering. The psychological effects were something else. They hooked onto my heart with a sadness which took over my dreams. It was a pain I could not share with Martin. I would have to face the loss alone.

Instead of giving birth my paranoia returned. I dreamt of a child. It was not clear if the child would choose to be a boy or a girl. The soul tagged along. A human face with a body of a kangaroo. The claws raked a rocky cliff while I labored uphill. The strange child laughed in delight while I wept. The little thing's umbilical cord was still attached to mine. On awakening from the nightmare I would have an intense desire to hold the baby.

I had never been at ease mixing personal issues with political agendas. My reflex was to see both sides at once, often merging somewhere in the middle. The universe perplexed me: everything had an opposite pole. "Make up your mind," Martin would say. "If you don't, then I'll have to make it for you." We would end up fighting. He would enrage me. I believed telling others what to do was unfair. How can we set a moral standard for others when the consequences are completely different for each and everyone? For days, months and years, I carried my unborn child in my bosom.

◆   ◆   ◆

Martin and I went back to Alec Rubin for a therapy session and a workshop of theater encounter.

It was like old times for me. I immediately lay on the mat screaming and kicking. I thrashed away in the dimly lit studio. Soft white tissues mixing with tears turned to fluffy balls flying around me. I was lost in my depression when I heard Alec directing us to work with a partner. I saw a shadow approach. Before I could tell who it was, I saw another dark figure flying up in the air. Instantly there was a commotion. A fistfight and shouts. Alec quickly flipped on the light. I sat up and saw a man holding onto his bloody nose and Martin hanging over him. "Man, I didn't know I wasn't supposed to go near your wife. I thought we were supposed to do theater games."

I was pained not flattered about Martin's jealous outburst. For me it was one more manifestation of the trouble our marriage was in. His actions made me turn away from him. I yearned for a stable life. I did not care for histrionics. I would like to trust Martin and have him trust me. I wished Martin could be strong and secure enough so he would care less about my interacting with another man. We were far away from the day he promised to take me where we could hide in the woods. It was the very spot he punched out my would be partner.

When our company was on tour, I would ask Martin to bring me a cup of coffee. He would remark, "You get to be the star and I am only a gopher." He still did not understand I did not wish to be a star. The stardom in my childhood nearly destroyed my brother, Ping, he felt so neglected and jealous. The stardom nearly destroyed me and my entire family. I never wanted Martin to feel we were unequal. I thought of my dancing friends and colleagues, as a child, how jealous they were of me. To shine on stage for me was to have some fun, to reach an energetic high. Yet, off stage my parents would manipulate that 'shine'. Jealousy was a noose: not only was I envied, but I too became envious of the others for their freedom.

From Alec's studio Martin and I walked in silence to the Roosevelt Island overhead tram. We no longer sang, 'hand in hand, looking for (the) god." We were alone in the tramcar. I held Martin's swollen face in my hands and kissed his face. He apologized, "I thought if family therapy wasn't helping, then back to primaling. Might do us some good." I choked up. Both Martin and I carried too much pain. Intimacy was too scary because we always got pricked by the other's thorns. Like Grandma said, "We are born to suffer." No, I want to uplift our spirits. A sense of desperation washed over me. I knew we were stuck in the pit. Would we find our way out?

Martin was a compulsive cleaner. He was annoyed by my messiness. He despised cigarette smoke so I decided to pick up my old habit of smoking. I spent most of my free time walking in the long hallway outside the apartment puffing the magic dragon. Feeling dizzy and unfocused, I believed Martin was going to kill me. I was certain I would not survive. Another time I was brushing my teeth in the bathroom, Martin came up behind me to give me a hug. I screamed in panic and ran shivering with fear under the bed to hide.

One evening I was soaking in the bathtub when Martin charged in, he was flying in heaven but dancing on earth. He had gone up to Woodstock to visit Kent, a dear friend. There Kent told him about 'Michael'. Martin had found a great answer, a medium named Shepherd who worked through 'Michael', not the archangel Michael who is said to be the keeper of the Book of Life i.e. the akashic records. "This Michael," he explained, "is a group of one thousand and fifty souls who have completed their physical cycle on earth. Michael works as a unit on the 'causal plane', the intellectual dimension directly 'above' the 'astral plane' which is the emotional dimension. Michael is the name of the last person who cycled off of earth." He spoke so energetically it was clear he was off on another psychic merry-go-round. It was distracting, even entertaining to watch him.

"Michael teaches we are eternal beings journeying from the 'source', or Tao, to which we'll return when we finish our journey on earth. On earth we choose one of seven roles: king, warrior, artisan, sage, priest, server or scholar. We also live through levels of soul ages. When we are cast down from Tao we begin on earth as infant souls, then we progress to baby soul level, then mature souls, last old …" Martin relayed as best he could what he had heard from Kent. Could 'Michael' help my present situation? I had my doubts.

I said, "I must be a down drudge baby soul-server serving you, the king, all day long." Martin was so excited he did not hear me. Or as Tysan would say just one of my Chinese jokes nobody understands. In spite of my skepticism, a week later we sat in Shepherd Hoodwin's studio apartment on East 62nd Street, talking to Michael through Shepherd's channeling. Martin discovered he was a 'mature server', which did not fit the image he had of himself. I turned out to be a 'mature scholar'.

We were led through a brief meditation while Shepherd channeled 'Michael'. He did rapid breathings; a penetrating glow of warmth permeated the room. Then 'Michael' in a deep voice, indicated to us to start our questions. Martin asked mostly about our relationship. Shepherd/Michael turned to face me. He asked me how I felt. I told him I was confused. Then Shepherd/Michael looked at me. I felt a shudder and gentle warmth encircle my heart. He said, "Welcome home. You've been lost for many life times, and now you're ready to heal your wound."

I had no memory before the age of fifteen. Primal Therapy had allowed me to cry out my needs and express my anger towards my parents. But I could not connect the feelings with a full conscious understanding. And so without conflict Shepherd/Michael became my teacher. I began to work with him on a weekly basis. I was used to the nether world. My childhood had been filled with such vis-

itations otherwise I might not have been such a ready candidate for guided meditations leading to past life regressions. The concept of progressive reincarnations
offered a formal system of personality categories which worked for me. I thought
it helped to explain our needs and proclivities as we lived out our lifetimes.
According to Michael the individual's essence remains the same through many
lifetimes. In this way we work out our neuroses, on our path to spiritual maturity.
This appealed to me right away. It gave me courage. I was comfortable not
doubting what someone else might have perceived as an unusual method.

◆　　　◆　　　◆

By now Martin had added a Masters in Theater Management to his Goddard
degree. I was still struggling with life. He seemed to be able to reach out more
easily. He had arranged a visiting artist audition for me at North Carolina State
University. I resented his preoccupation with 'good ideas' without consulting me
at the expense of our relationship. I had dropped out of family therapy once I
committed to Shepherd/Michael while he stayed on in private sessions.

"You can't change," I said. "You've no idea if North Carolina State will accept
me." We were on our way back to New York from the audition.

I could not grasp why my husband was sending me off to another state, alone.
It was true we were broke. Was I the only cash cow? Yes, our dance company had
been touring. Yes, we were professionally successful. But the fees we received and
the grants given to us were never enough. We had relied on Martin's parents to
help fund the company. Their generosity came with pitfalls. Martin's low self-
esteem was reinforced. In this way Judy and Irving remained super heroes who
controlled everything while he continued to be diminished.

I was reminded I could not speak English when I met Martin and he had said,
"It's a perfect relationship, Yung can't speak English, so we'll never argue." No,
we'll separate, just like what happened after our honeymoon in Taiwan.

"Why are we doing this again?"

"You'll not forget the past. I merely wanted us to separate for a while; I didn't
want you to abandon me."

"Huh? You don't make sense."

"We need cash."

"Can't you think of other ways to manage our lives?"

"Money is good. They'll pay very well for the work you do."

"Shove the money," I became angrier, "Why North Carolina?"

"What's wrong with North Carolina? Tysan can live with you. I can visit. You can expand your work. What's your problem?" A dark cloud circled. We were speeding along Highway 95.

"When I met you, you didn't speak English. You didn't argue with me ..." I opened the car door ready to jump. I needed to prove my anger.

"You're crazy!" Martin shouted, grabbing my side of the door.

"It's the same as before."

"No, I wanted to go back to school by myself. I didn't mean to separate. If you work in North Carolina for a year, it doesn't mean we're going to separate. You think you're the only one who has problems?" Martin barked.

I did not hold back. "You've got the problem," I persisted. I could see Martin was shocked by my belligerence. So out of character. "So what your father was dangerously ill when you were born? So what he was in the hospital for the first six months of your life? So what your mother freaked out when you were born?" I shouted, "Do you have any memory of this? My family was escaping tyranny when I was born. Their lives threatened by the revolution. You're the spoiled brat."

"You think you're not spoiled?" Martin yelled. "Look in the mirror, check yourself out. The world's not about you, either."

We continued to argue in circles. My heart ached. Martin had suffered from his parents' exclusive relationship which had kept the children out. Martin truly believed he was abandoned. Basically, we understood each other's needs. On the surface, we acted out our neurosis but we knew we would each have to face our individual demons.

The following day North Carolina State called to say I had the position. Five hundred miles away from home.

The faculty seemed to have respect for my work. They agreed to support whatever I wished to do. There was never any pressure. The opposite of home. For the first half year, Tysan came to live with me in a small town, Rutherford-ton, North Carolina. Later, she moved back to live with Martin. She was uncomfortable at school. I went back and forth, working for the State of North Carolina and our Dance Company and school in New York. Back and forth, for six months. I was living on highway 95.

At North Carolina I performed and choreographed for local schools and dance recitals. I was to take tea with local ladies. During one tea party, I dressed up in my Chinese Chungseng dress and exaggerated my eyes, more slanted than ever. In this way I would talk about Chinese culture and art. I was impressed by the women, except they confused Japanese, Korean and Chinese, or when they mistook 1920's Oriental Art Deco as genuine Asian art. They seemed genuinely interested in my talks despite my accent. I made it as clear as possible. I wanted them to understand as much of Chinese history as I did.

One afternoon I explained how a millennium before Christ, seven kingdoms divided China. Many great sages were born. Confucius, Loa Tze. Many other thinkers. Chinese philosophy and culture began to take shape and establish its unique roots. One of the kingdoms, Qin (300BC), united China. The first Qin emperor burned books and buried scholars alive. He built the Great Wall as well as his tomb. His son succeeded his throne but was thrown out by rebellion. The Han Dynasty came to power in two hundred BC.

In searching for a record of dance history in China I found texts which indicated court dances and rural folk dances. But no information on the origin of the practice of binding women's feet which would have ruled out the possibility of women dancers. Qigong and Martial Arts for men have a long history. There were no female players in Chinese opera in the past. Today male and female actors go through the vigorous eight to ten years of training, starting at the age of seven. A few reach the level of being a performer.

Another day I spoke of how traditional Chinese folk dances were generated in the 1940's after the Second World War. Many scholars and artists began actively researching and creating folk music and dance, partially for political agendas. Chinese folk dances became a way to teach Chinese people about our minorities such as Mongolians, Tibetans, Muslins and tribal mountain people. It was propaganda.

The popular Chinese folk dances in China and in the Chinatowns throughout the world are ribbon dances, fan dances, umbrella dances, DongHua Cave Deities dances, drum dances, handkerchief dances, dragons and lions, etc. Some of the styles, steps and formations look similar to 1930's Hollywood and Broadway musicals. While Mao was dead set against the capitalist Americans, I suspected his wife, Jiang Qin, watched Hollywood films in her bedroom behind closed doors. Whatever the reason I continued to enjoy "Chinese folk dances'. For me they were easy, fun and graceful. My audience rarely knew anything about Chiang Kai-shek. I explained he was Mao's rival. Chiang graduated from the Huang Pu Military School, working closely under Dr. Sun Yet-sen. He unified China after the Warlords tore China apart in 1920's and fought the Japanese War, which lead to the Second World War. His wife Madame Chiang came from a very prominent Sung family. The Sung sisters became the model Chinese females, one married to Dr. Sun and the other married to Chiang. When Chiang

Kai-shek lost his power struggle with Mao he retreated to Taiwan. The women assured me they were grateful to be so informed.

The following year, I did not continue the job at North Carolina. We returned to Roosevelt Island. The dance company had really taken off and this time we toured nationally. However, both Martin and I lived in whirlpools separated by our personal demons. I was terrified I would not be able to survive. Martin was tormented by his identity and career choice. We fought and fought and fought. Our relationship hit the rocks. The long forgotten childhood gnarling sensations crawled back.

We needed to discontinue the dance company. As successful as it was we could not make it profitable. I returned to North Carolina to teach the second year.

That year, Martin's father passed away. Martin's company laid him off. The Roosevelt Island apartment management threatened to evict him because he could not pay the rent. And then he pulled his life together. He found a job working for Minolta. He began to use his inner strength. However, I was still in my shit hole.

Martin began calling me in North Carolina to tell me I had abandoned him. A dismal and familiar refrain. How have I abandoned you? There was never any rational answer, and then one day I shocked Martin: I told him I wanted a divorce.

Martin continued to call Shepherd. He tried to show Martin a picture of my heart. My heart had a hole. He said, "An old wound." I was a wounded animal, I needed to go to the woods to heal by myself, and I should not come out until my heart healed. Martin asked Shepherd/Michael to persuade me to return to him. Finally, Shepherd/Michael said he must charge Martin for the phone calls. Martin was furious. But he stopped calling.

◆   ◆   ◆

My sessions with Shepherd/Michael intensified. The childhood memories began to bubble up mixing with glimpses of what I believed were past lives. I would take my pain to the North Carolina woods. My head hurt, my shoulders tensed up as if a steel prod had threaded itself through my back. I drank wine to numb the pain. I was also talking with a therapist at the university. I was so insecure.

I had regressed to childhood ways when Ping and I turned to the woods to cry for help. So I would lay myself down on the murky North Carolina dirt, inhaling the moist soil. I'd sprawl out on the ground like a lizard who sucked mold. I'd swing my tail side to side, giving power to my spinal cord. Earth heals me; heal my pain, my sorrow. I was a wounded animal lying alone in the woods hoping the howling wolf would turn into a teddy bear.

I cried to heaven and earth. I howled for help. I gathered stones in the woods and circled around them, dancing like a sorceress. I cast my power upward, downward, to the right and left. I purified myself within a magic ring. I walked uphill on a winding trail. The path ended by a lake. I sat by the lake and rested peacefully for a while. Then I felt dizzy. I shook my head in a violent motion. She appeared in front of me in a shimmering light. She was on her knees and crying. Her name was Satisha.

Satisha was a concubine of a sadistic Arabian king during the Thirteenth Century. She was tormented and tortured. She was chained to a stone column and not allowed to urinate for long periods of time. Her baby girl was taken from her. She was isolated from her family. Her master tormented her. She drank a poison that was intended to kill the king. Her spirit was broken. Rage possessed her. She wandered, weeping in a void of no man's land. She wept for her sorrow; she wailed for her pain; she howled for help and she too was lost in the crack between worlds. Satisha had come to me to share her darkened soul.

Satisha, don't weep. I'll join you to wander in darkness. Together we will roam through no man's land.

PART III

MICHELANGELO'S HEART

'To the Universe Belongs the Dancer. Amen'

Jesus/The Acts

Thirteen

It was a beautiful sunny January morning, with brilliant rays of sunshine coming through the window shades, I awakened feeling exhausted. My eyes were swollen; my tongue was coated, white and numb; my mouth was dry. It was 1991. My little cabin was situated on top of the Smoky Mountains. My life had fallen apart in a small town named Spruce Pine. I was so lonely.

Lying there in the sunshine with a warm blanket wrapped around me, I started to plan my day. I sensed this would be a very special day. Since I met Satisha I had made my mind up to turn things around. No more pain.

The moment I sat up I lay down again. Too much drinking. I felt nauseous. I pulled the blanket up to cover my head, which was throbbing. When I woke up the second time, I knew I had to go to the office. I was lucky to have a flexible work schedule. I staggered to the bathroom and filled the bathtub with steaming hot water. The washbasin, I filled with cold water. First, I plunged my face in the icy cold, and then I sank into the tub. I closed my eyes and breathed for a moment.

I managed to pull myself together. When I checked in at the college, Ann, the receptionist greeted me, "Hi! Yung Yung Tsuai ..." pronouncing Yung with a nasal twang. I smiled back. They must think I come from an alien world. The Chinese dancing doll from New York. I must hide my feelings ...

I had had a vivid dream recently. In my dream, my daughter Tysan's eyes were filled with tears. She asked me to come home. My little girl was begging me to return, because she needed me. Where is your daughter, now? Tysan was living with her father in New York. I was so far away. I went to the restroom and vomited. After everything cleared out of me, I sat on top of the toilet. I closed my eyes for a moment. Tysan's face was before me. Enormous, incredibly expressive and penetrating, her eyes were soulful beyond this world. People say a newborn baby cannot see anything. It was not true when Tysan was born, when I held her close in my arms. Tysan looked straight at me. Not only did she see me; she looked directly to my heart, to my soul. I was never able to forget Tysan's gaze. At the moment she was born as well as the moment she appeared in my dream, her eyes reminded me of coal-black crystal balls filled with joyful tears. She showered me with love and yearning. I wanted to love her, to take care of her, yet something had snapped in me. I had run away from home, from family ... but didn't Martin push me?

I sat with my right leg crossing over my left, shaking my right ankle in a nervous rhythm. I knew I wanted to get the day over with. No more pain. I left my office after a couple hours of fidgeting. I drove directly to a liquor store in the shopping mall. As usual, I stood in the center of the store, waiting.

Grandpa was an alcoholic; my brother, Ping was an alcoholic. My parents would not touch a drop of liquor. What am I? My mind ran its own course. Do I prefer red wine or white? Do I care? I like the feeling of blues after the wine soaked my body. Do I want to pretend to know about wines?

I lowered my head.

"I'm having some guests coming for dinner tonight. Can you recommend a nice wine for dinner?"

Be aware. I'm turning into a perpetual liar. I left the store with two bottles of Petit Paul French red wine, and headed for the supermarket.

At the pharmacy counter there were at least half dozen kinds of sleeping pills available. I was impressed. In New York, I did not notice any sleeping drugs over the counter. Is it my own ignorance? How did I not see them before? At this instant, the pills were everywhere. They waved at me. A cold fear set in my stomach, a shiver. I picked up a brand. Who cares?

I drove through the curving mountain road, facing the setting sun at five in the afternoon. I wept uncontrollably. I was drowning in tears ...

Time had slipped by fast. Tysan was a fifteen-year-old young woman. I hardly knew her ... I remembered when Tysan was five years old ... it seemed to be the same afternoon driving against a sunset, except Martin was driving. We were in the Catskills. Tysan was sleeping in the back seat. An exquisite, bright orange sunset hung against a dark thick cloud spreading across the sky.

Martin stopped the car, "Look! Tysan! Look at the sky!" Tysan opened her eyes, "How come the sky is so dirty?" ... Dirty dark cloud covered the blazing sunset. Dirty dark cloud entrapped the confused heart ... Ten years later, recognizing my skill in performing was not enough to replace my personal need for emotional maturation and expression. How could I develop? It was not enough to write my unhappiness in a journal as in my youth. Now years later I saw myself, once more, as a failure this time as a wife and a mother who had failed. The old misery had returned, gnarling transformed. This time my mother could not save me. By now I understood my creative worth, dancing and choreography maybe my life companions, but I had failed as a woman.

I stopped at the dry cleaner to pick up my skirt. The Chinese in New York ran most dry cleaners. Here in North Carolina, they also operated the dry cleaners. I wanted to lie down on the floor, curl up, so I could sleep right there. I had closed my heart.

Then, I drove to the butcher's. I ordered a thick juicy steak for dinner. Thinking of how the tender beef would taste. Steak, baked potatoes, topped with sour cream sprinkled dill, baby carrots cooked in sizzling butter, string beans sautéed with garlic and ginger, hot dinner rolls and a crispy salad. I wanted to wash it down with my Petit Paul French red wine. Maybe the hurt would wash away. Maybe I'll go to sleep, never to wake. I'll close my eyes and draw my last breath on this earth. Then, I'm going to have a date with my spirit friend, Satisha, in the netherworld.

"Satisha, are you waiting for me? Satisha, are you weeping with me? My beautiful friend, you understand me."

◆   ◆   ◆

I forgot about the vegetables and salad. I devoured the meat with the French wine and felt the violence expanding in my guts. I drank the rest of the wine. Nothing mattered. I took the pills out of the bottle and lay them on the table. I played a game of chess with those little white pills. I choreographed pill configuration. I hummed the Star Spangled Banner. I was elated that my misery was going to be over soon. I was going to take those pills so I could sleep in peace. But I was frightened. The world turned in spirals. I seemed to have no control over my actions. I was outside of myself. I saw myself dialing the numbers of the emergency room at Asheville Hospital. I asked to speak to my therapist Susan Sender but I was unable to reach her. So I asked help from the operator.

A woman's voice came over the phone, "What's your name? Where do you live? How many people are you living with? Who are your family members? What's your daughter's name? How old is she? Do you have pictures of her? What's her favorite color? What's her favorite song? I am glad she loves to dance. Do you dance? Do you dance together with your daughter?"

Questions pulled out of this woman's mouth like firecrackers on a Chinese New Year's eve. I was glad to answer the questions ...

"Now, would you do me a favor?" the woman asked me.

"Yes."

"Would you please take those pills and throw them in the toilet?"

"Well, I don't know ..."

"Would you do me the favor? I need you to throw those pills in the toilet and flush them down! Make sure you do flush them down!"

I did what the woman said.

"I will hold on to the phone while you flush the pills down the toilet, and then please come back and tell me more about your daughter, Tysan. What does Tysan mean?"

"Black Coral."

I saw the ambulance arrive.

"What's going on? I don't want an ambulance!"

"We are going to take you to the hospital and help you to sleep," the woman said softly, "I want you to bring your daughter's pictures with you. You may show the pictures to the nurses in the hospital if you want to. I am sure they will love to see her pictures. We won't hurt you."

I started to cry.

"Are you okay?"

"I think so."

"Can you walk outside your house to meet the nurse? She wants to share your feelings about your daughter."

The brilliance of the stars in the mountain sky shook me awake. I clutched Tysan's photos in my hands knowing the day was over.

◆   ◆   ◆

Mother! Hold me tight!
Let me taste the morning dew from your caress
Embrace me with your fire
Stroke me with your water
Nurture me with your passion
Blind me with your gentle whispering breath.

Mother! Hold me tight!
Teach me where I could reach the sun
Show me where I could find the light
Lead me the way this moment to eternity
How thirsty I am, how hungry!

Mother! Hold me tight!

Where are you?
I am terrified
My demons haunted me into the ground

It was during the peak of the October foliage. I drove up to New York from North Carolina. The red orange, purple, green, and blue landscape could not penetrate my heart. These sessions were painful. I was tense, trembling in my guts when I arrived at Shepherd Hoodwin's apartment. My upper body seemed pinched, a crumbled paper ball, my head screaming on top. There was no feeling beneath the ribcage, so I locked my knees together to prevent myself from falling further apart. I wanted this session to be over. I did not want to be there. I was far from any awareness. Perhaps the feelings compressed inside me since I was two years old were coming to an end? Now I was ready for liberation. Shepherd asked me to lie on the floor. He gave me a few relaxation exercises. Gradually, I allowed myself to sink within. My body began to expand. I was filling up space. There were no boundaries.

This is where my story begins ...
the root of my sorrow ...
This was the discovery of a shadow sleeping under the pillow.
There I was ...

It was pitching dark. I could not see where I was. My hands were tiny fists waving in the air; my toes curled. My buttocks tightened. I was crying. I saw Father's eyes, shining with rage. He was shouting at me, commanding me to stop crying. He brought me close to his body, and then he turned me upside down over a deep and dark cistern. The raven black hole shot way down reflecting his eyes. I was being pulled by the nothingness. I saw that death was manifesting through Father's eyes, hooking my spine, dripping the poison arrow of terror down my back. My breath was leaving my body.

"Pa Pa! Pa Pa! Bu-Yeou! Pa! Pa!' I was screaming in Chinese, "Pa Pa! Pa Pa! No! Pa Pa!"

His shadow covered my entire being. He was commanding me to stop crying. But I could not.

"Ma! Ma! I want Ma Ma!"

There was no hope. I was alone with this monster. With blood dotted eyes. The monster of the well was my father.

On Shepherd's apartment floor, my lips tightened, swallowing my breath. A numbed sensation under my nose. My shoulders stiff. And then I saw myself, I was two years old, and Father was indeed holding me over a well. He was threatening to throw me if I did not stop hollering. I had been living a life unconsciously waiting for my father to murder me with his rage. The child within torn apart by demons stayed two years old, struggling to be freed from Father's grip. I turned to Mother, asking her to soothe my pain. A dominating Father shook my nerves. A silent Mother created a void within me. I was bleeding in my heart. My worlds were split. Through a dark tunnel I went.

Five months passed before dawn showed her grace. I started to see the sunshine. My energy was clearing up. I was in the process of making friends with my rage, fear and sadness when the National Endowment for the Arts canceled its funding for the Visiting Artists program. I was out of a job. *'Cold, cold, cold, cold is all I feel …'* Mother's poem resonated in my heart. I was cold to Martin. I blocked out my feelings for Tysan. I had already made the move to end my marriage, blaming Martin. Of course, I made progress with Shepherd/Michael. But I was not able to reconcile my distrust of Martin. At the same time I considered it my weakness that our marriage had failed. I considered myself a bad mother. When Father told me about a job in Taiwan I did not hesitate. The next week, I was at the Taiwanese consulate office to sign working papers. I felt like a walking corpse, uncertain but determined. The director of the Cloud Gate Dance Company, Lin Haui Ming, had kindly extended a job offer. Lin and I had been friends in our youth. Suddenly, I was overcome by a kind of false sentiment: if I returned to Taiwan I might not feel so different. I'd belong. Paradoxically, I'd be 'home'. So I accepted Lin's offer. Within a month, and after a sixteen-hour flight, two hundred and seventeen passengers of which I was one arrived in Taipei. Hours later I settled in at an apartment the Cloud Gate had arranged for me. The next day I began to experience the independent life I had previously only imagined.

It had been years since Martin and I had honeymooned in Taiwan. I had finally exercised my right to choose at the expense of my family. Could this job in Taiwan work out? My heart swelled with hope or more appropriately with fantasy. Could I once again roam the bamboo forests? Would I be lucky enough to hear a fox song?

At the dance studio I observed bitter competition among the dancers. I watched in disbelief as people barked at one another for the least mistake. Was it Taiwan's financial success? The industrialization? I was used to positive interactions. Most of the dancers spoke the Taiwanese dialect while I could barely finish my sentences in Mandarin. This brought up the old demons of the Mandarins who grew up in Taiwan and the Taiwanese whose ancestors fled the Manchuria occupation. This disparity had remained unchanged. Long shadows from childhood began to cast unexpected darkness.

I would have to understand the student's psychological and social backgrounds to successfully be their leader. For this I was inadequate. I began to think they would suffer from my inability to communicate. How could they trust me? Was I helplessly stinking up the dance company like Ping when he accidentally fell into human shit, but here no one was laughing?

Now even the taxi drivers who drove me to work were hostile because I did not speak Taiwanese. It would be too much for me to be a failure in Taiwan. My perceptions of the environment were so negative.

I sharply recalled how I had missed so many opportunities to perform because I was too short even by Chinese standard. I was reminded of this fact almost immediately at the Cloud Gate. Fortunately, I was no longer sensitive to this. I had cultivated my skills as a choreographer. Dancers rarely have the skill to solve the puzzle of the music, movement patterns, staging and the many other components it takes for a dancer to communicate a story, a feeling, and an idea. Recognizing my choreograph skills had built up my confidence.

My head was filled with thoughts of Martha Graham: without our meeting I probably would never have left Taiwan. I came to understand the technique. At pain I had absorbed every nuance. Agnes De Mille the great American choreographer had described Martha as a genius. Agnes said, "Dance helps you reach out of the limitation of who we are—we can't fly, but we can try".

Martha knew how to fly.

I had spent three decades learning how to use Martha Graham's expressive technique. I learned to connect my emotions through certain muscular controls. The deep contraction/release and three-dimensional spirals were the fundamental concepts of the Graham technique. Out of these two concepts, she choreographed one hundred and eighty dances.

Martha had a larger than life reach, a gigantic shadow, and she had touched many people's lives. She had also influenced the history of American theater, commercial art as well as the fashion world. It was later I watched so many hearts broken, so many dreams shatter about her. Very often I fantasized about a solo dance I would perform when death finally visits me. In front of death I am able to stretch out my limbs, fly above the earth, whirl in circles, and howl like a wolf. In this dance I use the knowledge I learned from Martha. I am able to use the strength I had accumulated from her discipline to fight like a warrior. I am able to use the fluidity I practiced to outsmart the wrath of death. I am able to prove to Grandma I am no longer a little dead-slave girl. What would Grandma say now having crossed her river to the other side? What would Martha say? I knew I found no answers in dance, except, for the dance itself.

The fox is supernatural, mysterious, and other worldly, but ghosts belong to this world. It was not Martin or Tysan I was thinking about. It was Martha who headed my pantheon of ghosts. So much of her flooded my heart especially her soft resonant voice, "sing like a bird, fight like a warrior". I would need her courage to uphold my commitment to the job. Taiwan was feeling like a foreign land. Whatever flirtations originally had amused me quickly dissolved. Most nights I was on the telephone talking across the Pacific to Shepherd/Michael: *Why do we cling to habits which no longer apply? Are we so mechanistic? Can we ever shake our neuroses? Can we truly change? Our bodies seem to function according to the clock, but our minds run five hundred miles a minute. Why are we so possessed by those thoughts which separate us from who we are?*

I had trusted Shepherd/Michael to help me withstand my fears as I spiraled down the mind's rabbit hole. Maybe, it could have happened in another type of therapy, the pillar might have been successfully 'carved' and a sane Yung Yung could have emerged, but nothing worked. I had tried many methods none equal to Shepherd/Michael.

◆   ◆   ◆

I left my apartment at seven o'clock every morning. The ride lasted two hours through heavy traffic. The dance studio was on the outskirt of Taipei City. The company class began at nine. We proceeded with rehearsals, a short lunch break and then finished at six o'clock in the evening. Another two-hour taxi ride back, through honking horns and zooming sounds of motor scooters. By the time I went to bed it was ten o'clock. Six days a week. Sunday I did laundry and cleaned.

One day I received a letter from Martin informing me he was sending Tysan to Taiwan on her sixteenth birthday. The letter was like a needle on my skin. How much I had missed my child. I dragged myself out of bed and gobbled down a sugar bun with a cup of extra sweet, watery coffee. I was lucky to catch a taxi in the heavy smog. The driver skidded and wove through the narrow streets. As usual we pushed and honked our way through crowds, passing by tall apartment buildings and bustling stores through never-ending traffic jams.

When I looked out it was gray and dim. The city consisted of depressing cement buildings, one taller than the next. Taipei was becoming a city of international significance. For some people, it was a wonderful financial development. Was I stupid for desiring to see the rice paddies again?

Here I was on the island where I grew up and still loneliness showered me. I tried to envision myself draped in milky white chiffon floating midair in a dance of emancipation. For Tysan I would rise above my misery. I would create a duet to welcome her. We would move in unison. I decided Martin should join us. The trio weaved through different geometrical patterns, together and apart. A cello played, a flute sang, our hearts beat as celestial drums. We danced above the emerald isle.

I had anticipated Tysan's arrival so much so that when she arrived at the airport I smiled and stared at her as though I had never expected to see her again. She had grown tall and sensuous. The first few days Tysan accompanied me to the dance studio. At night we walked the streets. I showed her where I lived when I was her age. My childhood house in Yung Ho was gone. A plain apartment building stood in its stead. But Tysan enjoyed Taipei. With my daughter by my side I allowed myself to inhale the sweet scents of the night. In the past I had revealed so little about my childhood. Now I had the urge to show my daughter everything. The places I both loved and hated. I needed to share my Taiwanese past with her.

I began to miss our family in the old way. I did not share these feelings with Tysan. I did not know what to say. In truth Martin was my real family. Like my Chinese family, I pushed him out of my brain. I did not want to think about either of them. I was more disappointed with Martin. He did not know me. He did not care. I was to fulfill his needs, replace his emotional poverty leftover from his childhood. Tysan's feelings were not so confused. One night at the apartment she let loose, "How could you? How could you pack up, leave me? Without explanations?" Tysan paced about crying, "You're my mother. Don't you know I need you? Do you know I need you? Don't you know the pain you created?"

My heart ached. How could I explain how I believed she'd be better off without me? That I was not worthy to be her mother. That I thought I was protecting her by leaving. But I was wrong. Tysan did not measure me from any external, social point of view. She loved me. She simply asked to be with me.

I kept silent while she confronted me. When she finished I held her in my arms. I vowed, "From now on, I'll be there for you, you'll see, for the rest of my life."

Tysan fell asleep on my lap. As she slept I prayed to God to let me be a good mother.

The second week of Tysan's visit I hired a car. We traveled around the island sightseeing. We spoke very little but the silence we shared was precious. One day we were up early by the Mountain Hua Lian. A heavy fog surrounded the green mountains, like an ancient Chinese painting. Tysan said she could live in Taiwan, "Mom, it's a beautiful, mystical island." Was she saying she could live with me?

I had believed I was a nothing because I came from a small insignificant place. Traveling with Tysan showed me I had been wrong. Through Tysan's eyes I regained my sight, what I had prayed for, and I began to see the true beauty of the Emerald Isle. It was not just Taipei City, Taiwan was many things. It was also a land of fox song.

Shepherd/Michael suggested I could look up Terry Hu, that we had a strong soul connection. He explained Terry had accumulated great wisdom and love in this lifetime. She had been a famous film star who recently retired. She was currently devoting her time to translating the great Indian philosopher Krishnamurti's works from English to Chinese.

It took me six months to find her. By then Tysan had left Taiwan. The moment I called Terry, I felt the warmth in her voice. And she immediately invited me to visit her.

She cooked a delicious feast to honor me. Over dinner we talked. I began to feel good. She said she saw Krishnamurti's photo on the cover of a book and she was so moved by his face, she read everything available by him. Translating his books kept her in his presence. At one point I confided to Terry I had yet to connect with my dancers at the Cloud Gate.

"Do they pay well?" She asked.

"Yes."

"Then you shouldn't have problems. Think of a personality conflict as a learning tool for you, not a problem. Our inner 'hooks' must be released."

The next day at the studio I decided to let go of my little hooks about being judged. I stopped trying to prove I was worthy of being their teacher. I came to disregard my subjective discomfort with my students. I began to see the dancers' devotion to the dance. They were vulnerable and childlike in their hearts. It was still hard for me to watch adult men and women break down because they were told they were not up to the high expectations of the director. Like most dancers they put their lives in the director's hand and they gave their hearts to the art which predictably was universally underpaid and under appreciated. It was a familiar story no different in Taiwan. I came to admire them for what they did, and who they were. Tysan had helped to open my heart. And Terry helped me to see it was our cultural differences which made it difficult to find the right balance between friends and working colleagues.

My students could never be a replacement for family.

When the year was up I returned to New York, determined to secure my relationship with Tysan and reclaim my place in American culture. I had resolved this aspect of my life. But not my relationship with Martin. I needed to put a final chapter to the book of Yung Yung Tsuai and Martin Lerner: I was intent on a legal divorce.

I arrived without money. Fortunately, I was able to receive three thousand dollars from the Actor's Equity Union emergency fund. I was auditioning every day. One of the auditions was for the road tour of the musical Sayonara. I had first performed in Sayonara for the Paper Mill Playhouse years earlier when the choreographer was a young, blond, and beautiful dancer named Susan Stroman. (An artist who can dance and choreograph.) Her smile was sweet and her heart warm. She loved to wear a baseball cap. She never forgot a face. Ten years later I met her again when she was choreographing for the Graham Company, Susan recognized me and she gave me her warm smile. Another ten years passed, I met her again with the same sweet smile. Years later Susan choreographed and produced many successful Broadway musical, like 'Contact' and 'The Producers'.

Thankfully I got hired to tour. It would make me solvent. There was time enough before I left to pay a visit to Tysan on Roosevelt Island. She had requested I help clean her room. That was the pretense for the visit. Martin surprised us. He leaned against Tysan's bedroom door. He had cropped his hair short and was wearing a suit and tie. I had never seen him this way, not even at our wedding. He looked good. Gone were the jeans and the Jesus robe or a kimono or yoga shirt and pants. Now he really looked Western. His face seemed fuller, shoulders broader, waist thicker. At the end he could not help but flash his teeth, as he always did, announcing he must go.

We had not seen one another in two years. He seemed calm, quiet. I wondered about his relationship with his current girlfriend. Maybe, she was responsible for his new maturity? Tysan confided to me after Martin left that she would prefer to live with me when I found a place. The following week I met her at a West Village café. I found her sitting with Martin, drinking coffee and eating sweets. When I arrived Martin immediately got up. He said he had to go. I thought too bad. I wondered what it would be like to sit at a table as a family? Still, any recollection of when we were young and in love did not seem to melt my residual anger. He did appear changed. Was it a trick? To seduce me, only to slap me down again?

"We need to talk," he said before leaving. At my suggestion, we agreed to meet at a favorite Tea Shop Martin had introduced to me years ago. I had fallen in love with its variety of teas and teapots. I agreed. I thought a tea parlor neutral and civilized ground.

Fourteen

The day before I was to tour, we met on a bright Sunday afternoon. I was happy to see Martin. My heart beat rapidly. Was there anything in common left between us? I watched Martin, his eyes more green than brown, smiling, energetic, talking about his life. It occurred to me my asking for a divorce, my leaving had been a springboard for Martin to change. I did not have to feel guilty.

"How are you?" Martin looked at me with tender eyes. Maybe I could breathe easily in his presence.

"You know the year you left I hit bottom," he blurted out.

I took a breath waiting for his accusations. But they never came. Instead, he had a story he wished to relate. It was of a dream he claimed that changed his life. Martin became animated as he spoke ignoring his full teacup. "An eccentric couple appeared in my dream. I was attempting something. I can't remember exactly what but I wasn't being successful. They came up to me. The man in a blue flannel suit and the woman in an old fashion black and white polka-dot dress. They told me before I do anything further I must learn to 'spin the prosperity'. I asked them to show me." Martin stood up and demonstrated, moving his hands clockwise in rapid circles. His behavior stirred up some staring eyes. He ignored them and proceeded to demonstrate the dream's instruction to 'spin the prosperity'. I was laughing. "Yung," he sat down and took a sip of his brew. "Seriously, I've been prosperous ever since I started to 'spin my hands'."

What came to mind was the image of Martin at Alec's studio years ago when he spread his arms, leading a group of twenty screaming adults around in a circle.

"I'm still at Minolta but I've moved up," Martin said. "I'm doing well. I'm a good salesman in the company. I've found pals. Most of my co-workers are Irishmen. When I act proud because I've closed a deal, Pat circles his hand over my head 'shine the halo'. When I become bitter and competitive, he stomps his feet 'it's mine', like a five year old in the sand box. Rory likes to trick me, Eddy likes to tease me, and Mike always confides his crushes on girls to me. I feel I belong. We're all farts but I'd rather be a joyful fart."

Martin had become part of the ordinary world, and was at home with his new stability. I could never have predicted this transformation.

"Yung, even more amazing, some months ago I was walking down Broadway. At Eleventh Street, a couple appeared. I swear to you the man was dressed in a blue flannel suit and the woman wore an old fashion black and white polka-dot dress. They wanted a New York Times paper. I blew them off. Then in a second, I realized they were the couple in my dream! I chased after them, and led them to a newsstand, thanking them in my heart."

I thought perhaps Martin had experienced a lucid dream, but somehow he recalled the second meeting as a separate experience.

In the late 70's Martin had read Castaneda's books about his magical journey into the unknown. Castaneda had met an Indian medicine man, a Nagual, named Don Juan Matus. Under the tutelage of Don Juan, the young anthropologist entered another dimension where he experienced unusual glimpses of sorcery arts.

Martin had tracked down Castaneda's Magical Passes group. He had told me about these workshops. 'Tensegrity', a word borrowed from architecture, encompassing the words 'tension' and 'integrity', and this became the name for a set of physical movements Don Juan had taught Castaneda. In this way one accumulates physical energies as well as spiritual power. Other practices in these workshops were ways of letting go of past events, using techniques of breathing while moving head and eyes from left to right. Shifting head/eye perceptions was meant to help open the mind to lucid dreaming and other dimensions. Martin explained this was his spiritual path.

"I'm planning to go to Mexico for a workshop next month."

All of this seemed fantastical perhaps, except, I was talking to a clearly changed and stable Martin.

We fell in silence. Martin broke it, "Are you still working with Shepherd?"

I told him I had never stopped, even in Taiwan. I explained how the sessions were less emotional and how we were working with energy fields. And then, amazingly I felt completely comfortable with Martin, like an old, beloved friend. Who but Martin would understand my last session with Shepherd/Michael? I told him how during the session my mind went still. Waves of energy seemed to swirl in patterns. The experience reminded me of a Chinese spiritual, 'riding on the clouds, flying through the fog'. At the end of the session, Shepherd/Michael said it was interesting how my soul had chosen that moment to manifest. I had stripped away layers of muddy energy. I was ready to be on my own, to be independent. It struck me that Martin had discovered circles in his 'hand-spinning' around the same time I had witnessed my internal soul in a bubble of circular movements. A coincidence of wordless energies.

"Okay," Martin looked me in the eyes, "What about 'home'? You've just been home in Taiwan?"

"My heart is home. I don't know if I'll ever reach my heart?"

And then the new, stable Martin said, "Oh, you will. Yung, you will."

Familiar but different. I was there to discuss divorce. I had yet to contact a lawyer. I relied on Martin to take care of the matter.

"So, what about the divorce?" I said.

Martin went blank. Finally he said, "It's being processed through a mediator's office. I'll let you know."

I switched subjects. Tysan was working on weekends in a boutique. She planned to apply for colleges. "Maybe SUNY Purchase?"

Martin ignored the college subject. "She's gone through a lot the past three years. You were gone. I was a basket case. Sometimes I'd drive for hours to a deserted spot. I'd break down crying so hard. Sometimes at home Tysan cried because she didn't like the spaghetti I made her. It wasn't the spaghetti. She simply missed you."

How could I explain my guilt went with me everywhere? That I wondered if I would ever be able to make up for my actions? That it had been get out or die. I sat staring at the teapot. Then Martin spoke, "I didn't realize the pressure. The dance career was too much." He stumbled, "frankly, I didn't understand you were cracking up."

Silence.

Maybe I could not take the truth right there and then in the charming teashop. Neither of us ever knew how to pick up a broken conversation. So I asked, "How's your girl friend, Stephanie? Are you going out dancing? Cha Cha Cha, Cha Cha Cha …" I held my arms in a ballroom position.

"More like a Texas two step. Stephanie is okay, but we're breaking up. She's too young."

"Cha Cha Cha, Cha Cha Cha …" I laughed with Martin.

We exchanged good-byes at the subway station. Martin said, "It was good talking to you."

Hmmm, I watched his shadow disappear into the subway.

Still no divorce.

◆   ◆   ◆

My tour finished sometime at the end of summer. I resumed teaching at the Martha Graham and Alvin Ailey schools. Tysan joined me several times while I was touring. We were good with one another. She had developed into a gifted dancer. This helped us to bond. I began to teach her everything I knew. And, she revealed herself as a loving, willing student. And soon she was not only a professional dancer but a talented choreographer.

Martin had given up the Roosevelt Island apartment and had gone up to his family home in Harrison with Tysan. I also stayed with my parents. When he drove to work in New York he would pick me up at New Rochelle and drop me off at the Graham school. Working there was bittersweet. The original three-story brownstone building, which was given to Martha for her creativity and her lifetime work, had been sold to a developer and torn down. Now it was an ordinary apartment building like the rest of the business world in the City. Martha's school and studio sat in the basement of the building, sadly without its creative essence, as if Martha's resonate and beautiful voice was buried forever.

From time to time Tysan, Martin and I would meet up in the city after work. Like pals we ate out together. We chatted, laughed. It was pleasant, comforting. Nevertheless, I still believed a legal divorce would help end my painful past. Clearly, Martin had given up on the idea I would return to him. He no longer persuaded me or tried to talk to me about getting back together. And then the day we finally went to the mediator to sign the divorce papers it was I who broke down weeping, I could not sign. The mediator asked me if I'd like a few more days to think.

If I did not want to divorce, what did I want?

◆   ◆   ◆

At my parents' home I began to notice Mother's melancholy mood. At first I thought it was connected to my separation from Martin. Her excellent meals were punctually on the table. And then I realized my parents were not communicating. One night mother spewed out her rage. AnAn echoed her like a parrot. "Hwei Yee Lu! Twuan Hwo la ba! Papa yeo shei na ge bia tze! Hwai la wo men de quai la!" ("Memoir! What a disaster! Papa wants to write about that slut! And he ruined our happy life!") AnAn bounced around the room cursing Father. He did not understand what he was saying.

My father had kept a journal throughout his life. Apparently when he retired from his job at the age of seventy-seven, he decided to write a memoir. With a sense of his life waning, he wanted to leave something behind. Not Mother. He overlooked Mother's habit to sneak. She had no shame in the past. I remembered her words, "You're my family! Why should I not read what's inside of your head?

I can see what's going on. Mother of Heaven has got eyes!" she would pout her mouth and flip her tongue.

When I read Father's memoir, I felt removed, slightly disgusted, but mostly untouched by his sentiments for Teacher Li. I understood his writing was a release from his guilty conscience and burdened memory. Hardly a memoir for his children. It vividly brought back my childhood curiosity about his eagerness to be at Teacher Li's studio, and of course the mysteries of sex.

Mother's main focus fell naturally onto her family. She did not function easily in America without Father's assistance. Father was the central figure in her life. She was curious about his writing. She claimed she did not read his first book. However, when he went to Chinatown to teach his weekly Tai-Chi classes, she secretly read his second one, which told the stories of the life they lived after they moved to Taiwan.

I approached Father, "What's the matter?"

"Aiya! Your mother read my memoir!"

"What?"

"I wrote about my affair that happened forty years ago …"

"So?"

"Your mother can't read it. She shouldn't read it …"

"Why?"

"It's about Teacher Li Sui Fang. You know …"

Thunder and lightening. I did not know. Of course, it was clear. I had smelled something wrong when I was ten years old. And suddenly I felt betrayal along with Mother. The shimmering vision of Teacher Li's nude body. The strong odor of roses had not been a child's hallucination.

You said you were simply trying to make me a star. You were so thrilled! You claimed you cared about my dancing career. You were never home for Ping and me, but you shaped my life in the dance world. I confronted you in my letters about your relationship with Li and you denied so vigorously. You broke down and cried so hard after you read my letters, that your emotional response caused both Ping and Mother to withdraw from me for many years. They even called me a "Red Guard"! But why do you have to dig up old worms now?

Mother looked frail. She was suicidal for the next two weeks. She would not eat or drink. She cried. All the old issues came up. She beat herself up hard, making blue and black marks everywhere on her small body. She struck Father across his face with all her enraged strength. She cursed her deceased parents for abandoning her. She blamed her great-grand mother's ghost spirit for spoiling her as a child, only to be humiliated and taken down by my evil father. She spat at her dead aunt, who introduced her to Father when she was seven years old. She raged at her late mother-in-law and Father's cowardice when it came to our circumstances in Taipei. Most of all, she was devastated by the insulting betrayal written in my father's journal. She read of his lust and passion for his lover. His wonder eyes for Li spilled onto the page like a poisoned serpent, eating at her heart, word by word. She exclaimed to me, "Your dance teacher, I suspected adultery at that time but did nothing except lament in secret darkness. I even bowed to the woman because I needed to thank that cheap slut for your dancing future. Yung Yung, I can't recover from my grief, I can't forgive your father."

A few days after her discovery of Father's memoir, she decided to pack up and go back to Taiwan to enter a Buddhist temple. She wanted to become a nun. I called acquaintances on her behalf and tried to find out which temple was suitable. I was told none of the temples would accept a seventy-five year old woman. Besides, the nuns must live together, work very hard from dawn to dust. If Mother thought her life was hard, she had very little idea how tough a nun's life could be, especially, since she was not at all religious.

I did take her to visit a Zen monk somewhere in New Jersey. They talked about her situation. Mother was embarrassed. She rejected the Zen monk as someone who had no depth of understanding life. In fact, she was a little fearful. How can a monk understand an ordinary person?

On the way home she said, "Oh, he told me sometimes things happened because of a karmic situation. When I asked him what the karmic situation was, he had no answer. I think he was trying to swindle some money out of me."

Mom! Don't you see he does not want your money? Don't you see he tried to help you, but he could not? Don't you see he saw you were not open to be helped? I wanted to shout at her stubborn deaf ear. Mother, I want you to change, to become a strong and more intelligent woman. Mother, Your pain now is my pain. It is crunching in my stomach. Don't disappear on me! Please! Stand up to Father! I need you to be here for me. I need you to wipe out the traditional Chinese women's fate and turn the world around. What if, as Maxine Hong Kingston suggests, Chinese women were once so dangerous, their feet had to be bound?

I held back, Mother would have been frightened by such a brainstorm. "Mom, if you could change, and be indifferent to Papa's doing you will be setting an example for your granddaughters and me. That would be a great karmic relief, if Chinese could treat their women differently after a thousand years of abuse."

I choked up when I lectured my mother. She pinched her face and pouted in her way. We fell into silence. No more talk about being a nun.

And no more talk about changing. How could I ease my parents' pain? I concluded they did not know how to live out their lives gracefully.

Father's regret for writing the memoir was driving him mad and everyone around him. They were drowning in despair.

Mother had torn out a page from her old diary, crumbled it into a tight ball and carried it around for days. She kept it in her bosom. When she showed it to me, she unfolded it so carefully as if it were a treasure. She had written her unhappiness forty years ago to prove how her heart was broken. I recalled the incident, over a bowl of Wanton soup. It was when Teacher Li came to our home to borrow money to set up another dance studio. It was when her husband had gambled away their house, the school and their savings. Mother served her a bowl of Wanton soup, which Teacher Li did not finish. After she left father picked up the bowl and finished the soup with savage, lusty eagerness.

"Why do you finish her soup? You refuse to touch your own children's leftovers?" And indeed father began his secret affair with Teacher Li the day after that visit.

For generations we were taught how to behave as Chinese women. Everyday we were told, "San Tsun Tse De ("Three obediences and four virtues") "Obey father as a child, obey husband as a wife and obey sons as one gets old." We were taught how to repress our feelings for our virtues. I wished Mother could change her consciousness, see the helplessness of her stubbornly blinded small vision of the world. Mother's heart had been wrenched as she identified herself with certain traditional writings to depict the role models of a Chinese female. A typical style of Chinese writing about flowers, rains, winds, moons and loneliness.

How I had wished my parents were different. How I had wished I lived in a different world. In both their journals it was all circled around my dancing. "It was for Yung Yung's future!" Father's excuse. I recalled now he had stayed at the studio when a typhoon hit Taipei. Mother was alone nailing down windows, securing our possessions by stacking them on a wooden table that could float if our home flooded. Ping and I were sent to the local high school complex with candles, flashlights and canned sardines. Mother had had futile arguments over safety issues with Grandma, who sat on a wooden board refusing to leave home. Where was Papa?

Father wrote about Teacher Li's luxuriant body and his lust for her. How she would be willing to be his mistress if his wife permitted. How he felt guilty because he knew Mother would never be at peace if she ever found out … Clearly he could not forget his mistress and now Mother could not forgive him.

Father ceased his writing of the past. Mother no longer served him. They argued. Caring for AnAn became their one link. Like AnAn said," Why can't we laugh and have fun like the way we were before? Why did you have to write the story about that slut? Why did you have to write your memoir? What a disaster! Can we turn the time backwards and live together again in a loving way?"

Can they? Can they pull back the spilled beans and realize sky is blue and sun does shine? I saw my parents as a fragile aging couple with a brain damaged child. It was all very separate from my life. I thought. But the clouds had not blown over. I called Shepherd/Michael who was in New York. I told him I was ready for a past life regression therapy session. It took little time before I found myself barefoot squatting on a dirt ground in tattered robes by a hut where we lived. I watched a little boy play in the mud. I looked at him with a pinched heart. I felt he was my son. Everything he did annoyed me. I watched him playfully jump over the mud hole, as if he had no worries. I think he does not know he is an untouchable! Look at him. His face, feet and arms filthy. I am going to make him stop laughing. I am going to threaten him, so he will stop laughing. I am going to make him feel like me, a pathetic worm. I wanted to hold him upside down and shove him down the mud hole. A surge of hatred rushed from my gut to my throat. I yelled out and commanded him to stop laughing. He looked up. His eyes reflected my eyes, dotted with black anger, shining with rage. There was the terror. There was the hatred. There were my father's eyes. And there were mine. The images were vivid. Father and I played out our roles in reverse. He returned a negative emotion back to me as I did once to him.

After the session, I went home and lay down on my bed. I allowed myself to exhale for a long moment. How do I feel about Father? I answered my own question with a faint smile: there was no difference between us. I was swimming in the slightly warm, pinkish glow of completion.

Fifteen

The Christmas holidays were upon us. I had been asked to teach the Graham technique as well as to create a repertoire piece for a private dance school in Torino, Italy. It was a six-week workshop and well paid.

The Philippine brother and sister who owned the Torino Dance Company kept me busy. During the day I was occupied with the dancers. At night I played therapist to my disgruntled employer. He tended to lament over many glasses of wine, how his sister did not understand his homosexuality. It was well worth it. We were close to the New Year. Soon I would be realizing a life long dream of visiting Florence. Three days of bliss. I was going to give myself a present: I had dreamt of viewing the original Michelangelo's David since childhood.

I boarded the train early New Year's Eve, December 31st, 1993. Arriving to find my sparsely furnished room poorly heated. I could think of nothing but what awaited me the following day. I finished off my last sausage sandwich congratulating myself I had actually made it to Florence, Italy when I heard loud screams and bellowing, followed by a cacophony of unidentifiable mayhem. It sounded like a continuous crashing of falling objects. Pandemonium. Was it the end of the world? I trembled wondering what to do next. I made my way to the tiny lobby where I found the porter drinking directly from a champagne bottle. "Buon Ani," he handed me a chipped plate and demonstrated how to throw it out the window. He saw my stunned expression and explained how the Florentines traditionally threw out all their chipped crockery at the stroke of twelve, to welcome the new year.

By morning there was not a shard on the street. Without a guidebook I made my way around the city. I bought food in outdoor markets. I ate, sitting on a bench in a Piazza. January was not a tourist month. I could not imagine how I appeared to the locals. I figured they were used to foreigners.

At the Duomo I walked along the festive multicolored marble, pink white and green—at the tribune I viewed Michelangelo's Pieta. He had included himself as an old man standing above the Virgin and Christ. His face incomplete. Intended for his own tomb, the Pieta was hacked up by the artist himself. The tale goes, a rage overcame Michelangelo. When his anger subsided there was damage, but the head of Christ remains an extraordinary expression of suffering and beauty. An expression of a higher being coming through his eyes, a sense of acceptance on his lips, or is it his comfort resting in the hacked arms of the Virgin? I wondered why Michelangelo damaged his work? Was it anger at his eventual death? That his creations should outlive the creator?

I was transfused with the taste of genius. I walked along the narrow cobblestone alleys, imprinting my footstep. Many Florentines believed spirits rest within the statuary. I, too, experienced the statuary as alive, not as flesh and bone but as appearances eternally manifesting sacred beauty. I spun from one masterpiece to the next transported by the silky marble. I was equally awed by the nude David at the Piazza Della Signoria and the Piazzale Michelangelo. (The original David was in the Academy.) It was said Michelangelo portrayed David at the moment he was ready to fight. ("Sing like a bird, fight like a warrior," Martha's mantra.) Nothing could impede my perception of the godlike gift of Michelangelo. No matter what I learned of him: his not bathing to the point of flesh peeling off when removing his garments, or his rejection of women, none of this altered my sense of the sacred majesty of his creations.

Once at the Della Signoria I stayed with the David for a long time. I felt I was in the grip of a great beating pulse. Why am I so excited? So happy? So unafraid? Michelangelo's heart and mind, so idealized, enthralled me. Each day I returned to my little, scruffy hotel, my soul filled with riches. Something I lost was recovered in Florence: a sense of the world's beauty.

Florence smelled of ancient unyielding stone. Buildings stacked stone by precious stone, angels intricately carved waited under rooftops and along walls. Never did I feel more protected. The water fountains sprouting well water caught rainbows which richly reflected off the stone. I had imagined intense odors of garlic and pasta. Instead my senses were overwhelmed by stone, and marble. I fantasized an apprentice of the great master, also searching for the ideal, willingly hauling the marble, so gods could appear to man.

I was in awe wherever my eye took me. But it was always Michelangelo. I would walk from Piazza to Museum to the Duomo and back, in the grip of a supernatural vibration, which I came to believe, was Michelangelo's heart. How could I reenter the ordinary world? That night intense yearnings overcame me. I was restless in my bed desiring love and to be loved. But by whom? The answer came in the middle of the night.

In Chinese mythology, a god named "Peng Gu" created the universe by stretching his body, his arms holding up the heavens, his feet grounding the earth downwards. In this way heaven and earth could never be separated. Peng Gu visited me. It was a holographic image. He hovered over me. I was not afraid. Then he removed his mask. It was Martin smiling, opening his arms to me. My body trembled. I called out his name. I felt my being merge with his image. Can you hear me Martin? I love you beyond any intellectual understanding. Every desire raced through my body, my heart, a giant gemstone, radiated out to the heavens. What universe could I reach with my love. Martin was the only person with whom I could travel this spiritual journey. And, we were already halfway there.

There is a Han Dynasty folktale called 'The Diplomat': "A tiger, a wolf and a fox who went hunting together, caught a goat, a rabbit and a chicken. Soon after, they sat down to discuss how the spoils should be divided. The tiger was thinking, "I could eat all three by myself." But he pretended to be fair, and asked the wolf, "How the spoils should be divided? What do you think is fair and square?' "O, big brother," the wolf replied, "you're the biggest, so you keep the mountain goat. I'll have the rabbit. Let the fox eat the chicken." The tiger was very dissatisfied and became angry. The wolf was so scared that he ran away lest he become the tiger's next meal. Turning to the fox, the tiger asked him, "Fox, how would you divide the three?" "O, King of the forest," the clever fox answered, "you're the biggest, so you could have the chicken for your breakfast, the rabbit for your luncheon, and the goat for your evening meal." This was what the tiger wanted to begin with and it pleased him so much that he asked the fox, "Where did you learn to divide such fair judgment?" "I learned by observing what happened to the wolf," the fox said. Thereupon he also ran off as fast as he could.

I, too would be a savvy fox. And, as quickly as I had run from the responsibility of loving I was flying back to Martin. It was he who had struggled to help me uncover one therapy after the other in the hope I might be healed. He persuaded me to continue with the dance. He introduced me to Shepherd/Michael. He found a home for me.

My face was wet with tears on the flight to New York. Tears of relief, with a tinge of fear. What if Martin had other plans?

I arrived at my parents' house wondering if they had killed one another? Mother and Father appeared cool not hostile. A good sign. Mother retained a martyr's air but was no longer desperate. Emotions had neutralized.

She greeted me with an urgent message from Martin, I was to call him on arrival regardless of time. And so I rang Martin at Harrison. He said he had something important to tell me. Oh what could that be?

No. He had to see me.

The next morning Martin came to pick me up. I was shaky. I did not wish to show any emotional signs. I wore a lot of make-up so he would not see through me. He asked why I was so made up? I explained I wanted to look a certain way when I auditioned. I wore a necklace of Italian coral as a sort of talisman. We were quiet. I waited for him to speak. The morning rush was the usual parking lot. I was not in a hurry. Martin spoke first. He said, "I had a vivid dream." He took a deep breath, "you came to my room. You were weeping," he said, "you came to me for comfort."

Yes, yes, I thought. And, right away I saw there was no need to relate the extraordinary visit he paid me to the dingy hotel room in Florence. We had virtually the same dream. And, this was the beginning of our recognition that we would be together for the rest of our lives.

I had this idea about a wedding. In my mind the first wedding was for my visa and I was not ready to be married even though we did live together. The second wedding I was six months pregnant with a watermelon stomach. I still did not feel ready. Martin's parents made all the decisions and invited their friends. Judy was actually more the center of attention. This time, I wanted it right. Martin went along with me. We asked Shepherd/Michael to lead the wedding ceremony. So we said our vows on my birthday September the 8th, 1994.

We were re-married at our newly furnished apartment at 11th Street and Broadway. I had found an off white dress made of lace in a thrift shop. It was very feminine, very beautiful. A tailor put in a satin lining and the dress felt luxurious against my skin. I carried white roses and pinned one to my hair. Tysan witnessed our exchange of vows as Shepherd channeled Michael to give the wedding ceremony. "Behind the rage is the power; behind the fear is the courage, behind the sadness the joy.' It was a simple, quirky wedding but it was mine.

We spent the night at our apartment. At first we were both shy. It had been a long time. Now my husband was learning to reconnect with me, and I with him.

The next day we invited fifty people to our wedding banquet at Zen Palace. We served vegetarian Chinese food and a three layer white wedding cake washed down with champagne. Judy and my parents were among our guests.

◆   ◆   ◆

On one of our frequent drives out of the city we drove upstate to Oneonta. Weaving through Rt. 28, passing Woodstock, Phoenicia, Pine Hill, and turning onto Rt. 30 from Margaretville lead us to a very handsome town, Roxbury tucked in the midst of the Catskill Mountains. The Victorian houses lined the streets told of a prosperous American history as the Dutch explored upstate New York in the early 18th Century. There were two gas stations, a school, a library, a video store, Taste Bud Luncheon, a bank and a church made up the town. The stone church, built by Jay Gould's family, stood a shining beacon in the middle of the town. Its Tiffany's stain glass windows gleaming as jewels. Separating 'our town' was a haunted graveyard rich in memory drawing the line between the trailer parks and the elegant old town houses.

Early next morning we drove from our motel to an empty house made of logs to sit by the porch and watch the sunrise. The log cabin was a fifteen-acre farm-land for sale. The rumor was the Dugan family who had owned the two hundred acres of dairy farmland during the Sixties raised marijuana crops. One day heli-copters flew over the land. Soon the State confiscated everything.

We sat on the porch in the sunshine. Martin imagined planting fruit trees. There were already magnolia, birch and pine plus a willow tree dreaming by a pond. We found our 'home'.

◆   ◆   ◆

Father's manner had changed since Mother's discovery of his memoir. When I rang them, he would hand the phone to Mother. It was not a natural thing for him to do, as he was so used to being the center of attention. Now he encouraged me to talk more to Mother. He created space for us to relate to one another. The world no longer revolved around him. In general, he listened to me and I could listen to him without reacting.

As Shepherd/Michael once said to me, "Welcome home," the home I had longed for was never the home Father and Mother had talked about. It was the soil of the mountain I stood above and the waterfall I swam under. Whenever I invited my parents to follow me down the yellow brick road to our beautiful log cabin they would refuse. So different from their first look at America when they were so eager to see whatever I brought to them. In Central Park they had sat as children in a carriage drawn by a black and white horse. I joined with them in their gleeful reaction to the Radio City show at Rockefeller Center. It had been a unifying moment of laughter and joy. This time they were not only refusing to see our mountain home, they added they were afraid of the mountain's spirits.

I knew they were interested to find plots for their final resting place. With this in mind, I suggested they travel to Roxbury to view land. It had been two years since we had bought the Duganhill property. This time the autumn tiger's oppressive heat helped get them there.

A four hour trip took the Tsuai family eight hours. When we arrived, it was night. Father, Mother and AnAn timidly stepped out of the Honda. They were immediately awed by the stars spread over the mountains. They danced like little children by the pond. Father waved his arms, pointing here and there; he swayed and bowed. Then in a flash Mother lit up a cigarette, she dashed, forward and back, she promenaded in figure eight circles. AnAn threw himself on the grass field; he rolled and twirled. They were carried away by the power of the mountain at night.

Father looked up. He pointed out the stars to Mother, "Kang Lin, look! We haven't seen such a starry night for over a decade. I almost forgot how beautiful the sky looks at night."

Mother pouted. And then she shyly smiled.

Father stole a glance at Mother and smiled, 'Look! The big dipper! The Milky Way! Look! The cowboy star and the weaving girl star!"

"Pa! Mom! Look! We call that one the North Star," I pointed my fingers in the same fashion as Father was doing, with his gestures grand and dramatic.

Martin joined us. He looked at me in an expectation of a translation, "Look! Over there! The Venus Star!"

But I dropped the ball. I did not know how to translate "Venus" in Chinese.

AnAn picked up the cue, "Venus Star! Venus Star!" He spun and spat out the English words, which sent Father and Mother into a gale of laughter.

At that moment I fell into a dream.

Universe rotated infinitely. Father, Mother, Grandma, Ping, AnAn, Martin, Tysan, Martin's parents all danced among the stars against the rich velvet-night backdrop, each one of us had a Fox song within us. The silvery shimmering spider web of the galaxies connected us. The pain had gone, so had the anguish, the struggle, the contradiction, the friction, the bigotry, the battle, the war.

When I came to, I saw my family, like adorable lunatics, still pointing up at the sky. And then I watched as they cavorted down the mountainside, their forms indistinguishable from the earth. And, there it was: The Dance of Life.

1996

After Word

The mind plays tricks. Things, which happened fifty years ago, feel like today. It has been suggested if we were able to reach beyond our ordinary perceptions we could see our past lives form, not by the linkage of time, but by a thread of common themes. That we live in spirals driven by unresolved issues, rather than, clocks and calendars. That the mind places our thoughts in an order, which contradicts our daily reason. And this could be called a cosmic joke.

When I try to define who I am by looking at where I grew up, when I was born, etc. my being speaks very little with the logical identity. My recollection of experience seems to cluster in different patterns outside the time we humans have created for ourselves. For example, I can still hear the Fox Songs my grandma sang to me: they ring fresh and clear, like the very first day I heard them.

978-0-595-47325-0
0-595-47325-3

Printed in the United States
97762LV00005B/223-249/A